Watercolor Faces

LEARN TO PAINT VIBRANT, EXPRESSIVE & FUN PORTRAITS

by Anna Nadler

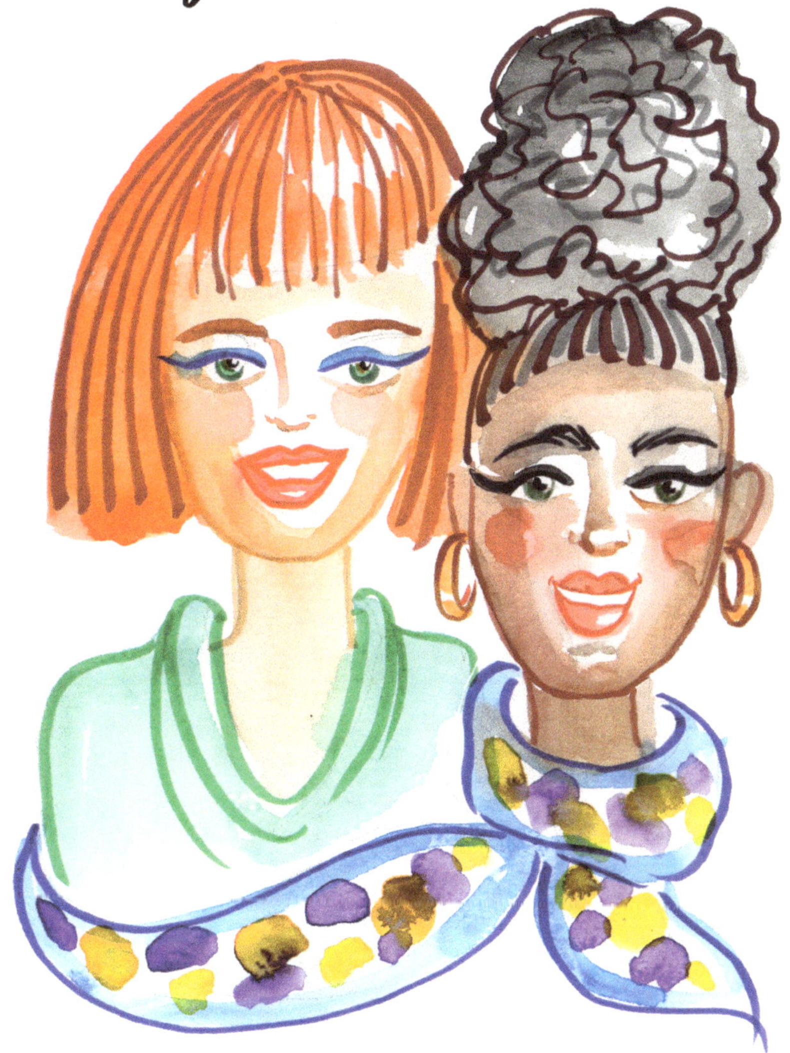

ISBN: 9781958428450

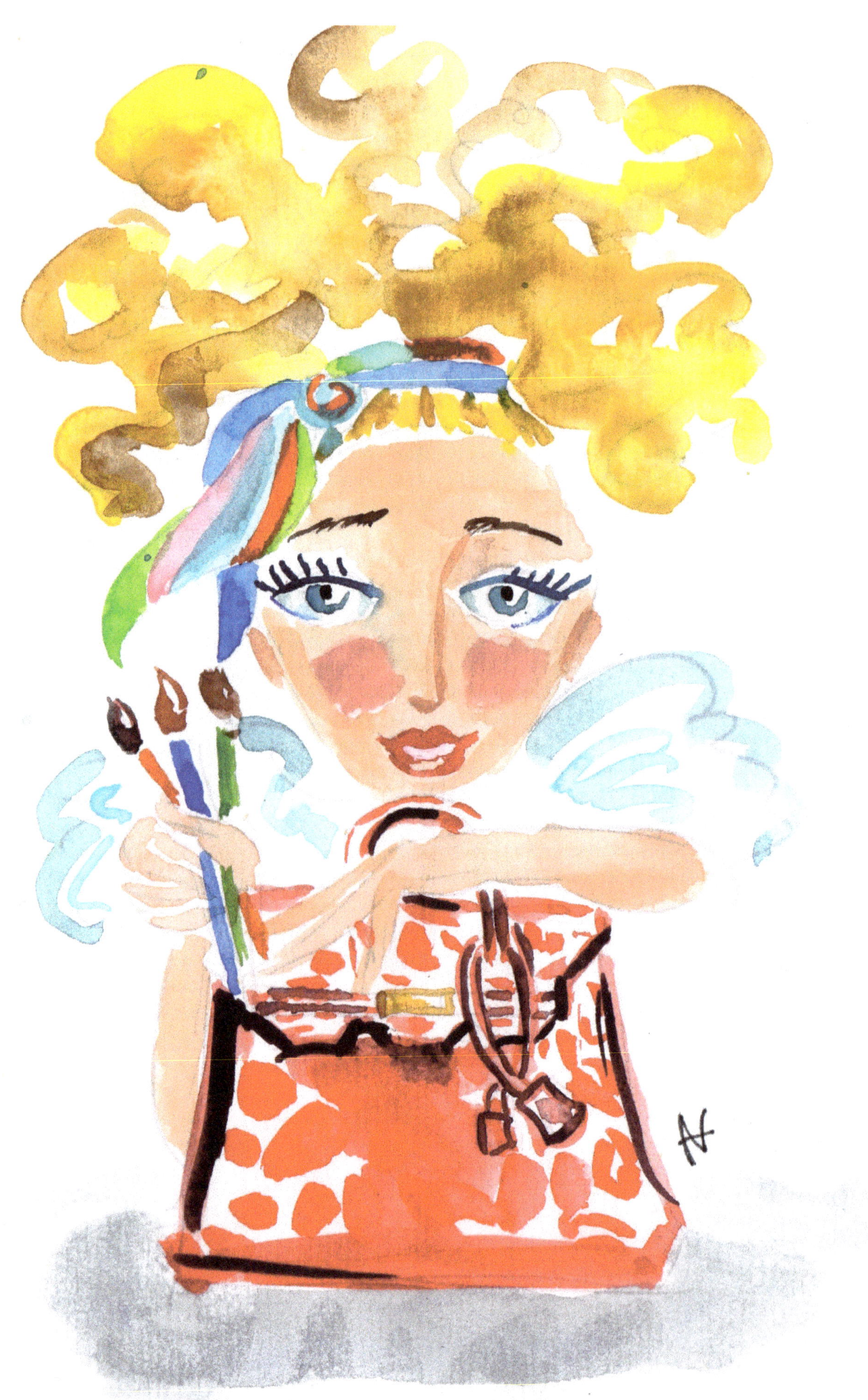

Table of Contents

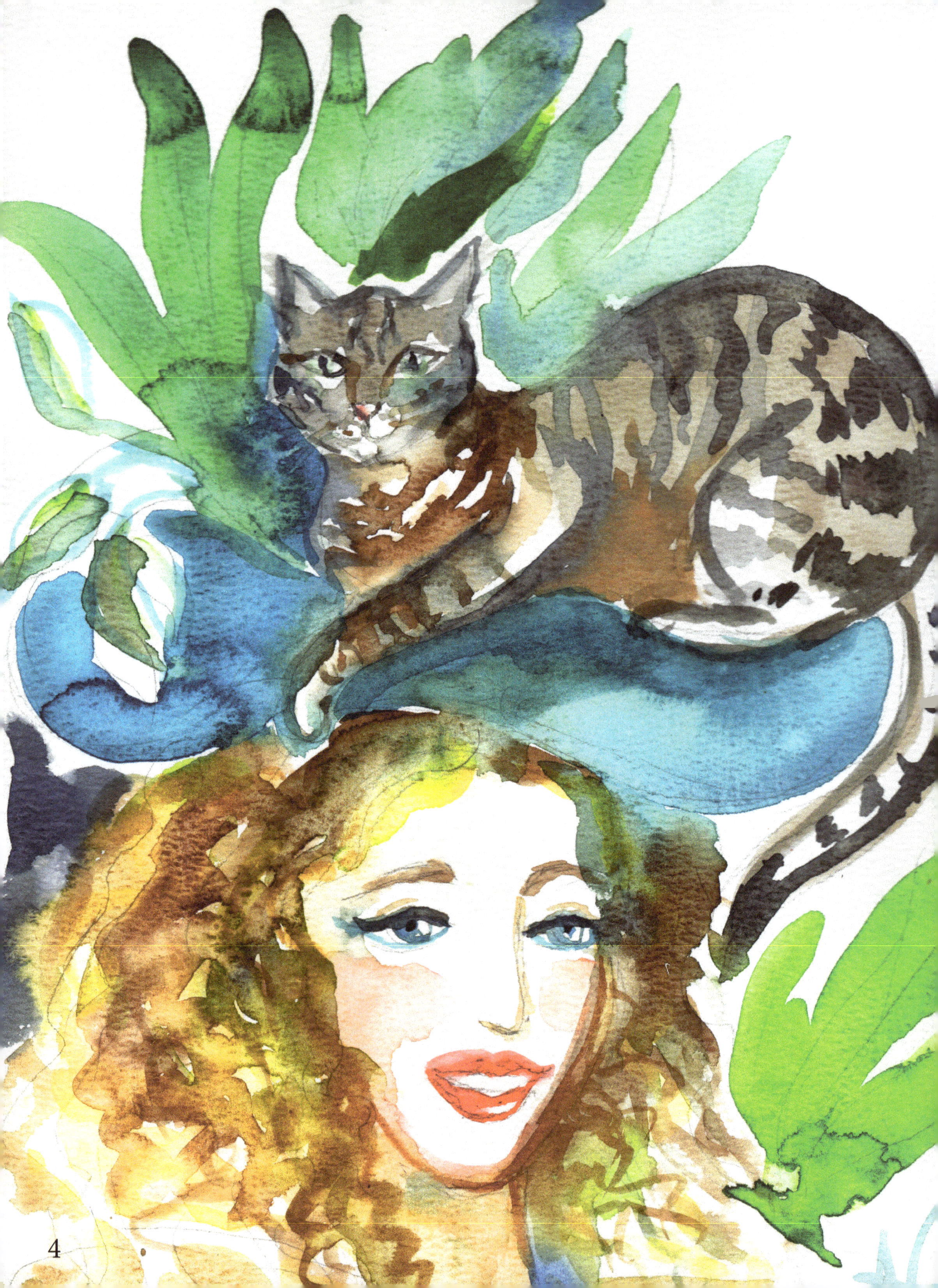

Introduction

Dear Artist,

Welcome to this fun volume, which is all about painting faces in watercolor. We will cover various ways of creating face illustrations, in simple, as well as more realistic styles.
We will paint from illustration and photo references.
Every drawing and painting exercise has step by step illustrated instructions.

We will go over different mediums to use in creating your portrait illustrations. By the end, you will feel more confident in using the medium of watercolor, as well as other drawing mediums, to create your face illustrations.

This book is not a stiff or verbose instruction guide, rather it is a light and friendly approach, that is open to beginning artists, as well as more experienced ones who are looking to practice their face illustration skills.

The book starts with basic principles of facial anatomy, going over male and female face shapes. Then it goes into painting facial features. We will experiment with painting straight away vs sketching with a pencil, as well as using pens and various markers. We will explore painting from photos, as well as create imaginative conceptual portraits from our imagination.

I hope you enjoy this book as much as I have enjoyed creating it! Please also check out the other watercolor and marker illustration books in this series!

Art Supplies

You can use any brand tube watercolors of your choosing. There are many great sets available on Amazon and other online retailers. The set I use has 30 colors in total.

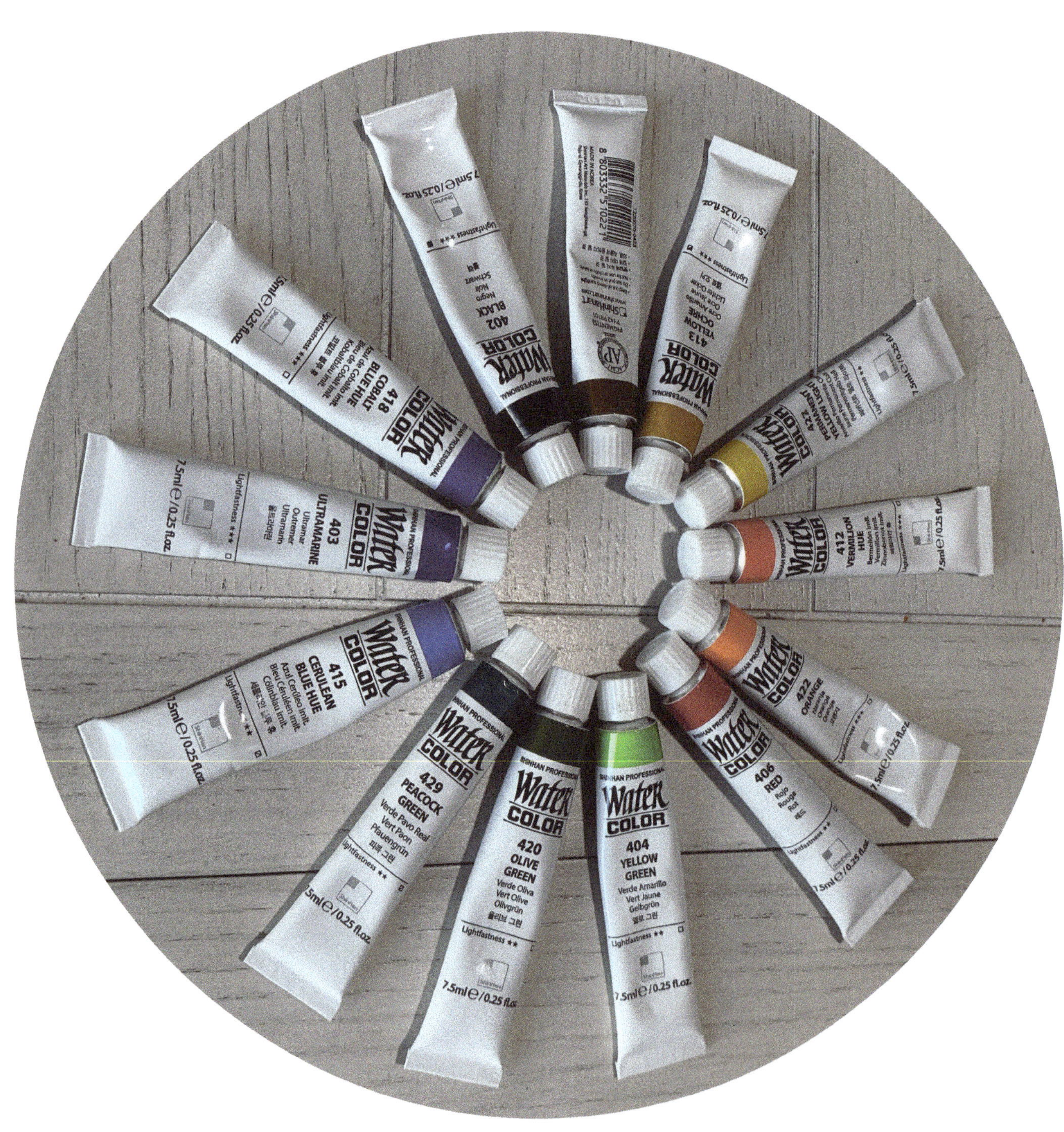

Along with your tube watercolors, I recommend you get a metal tin pallet, where you can squeeze out the colors you wish to use now and in the future. Even when the pigments dry, they keep indefinitely, as they can be activated by using water.
I also like to use good quality synthetic watercolor brushes of various thicknesses. I also always have paper towels nearby, to dab off any extra water as I paint, as well as to fix mistakes.

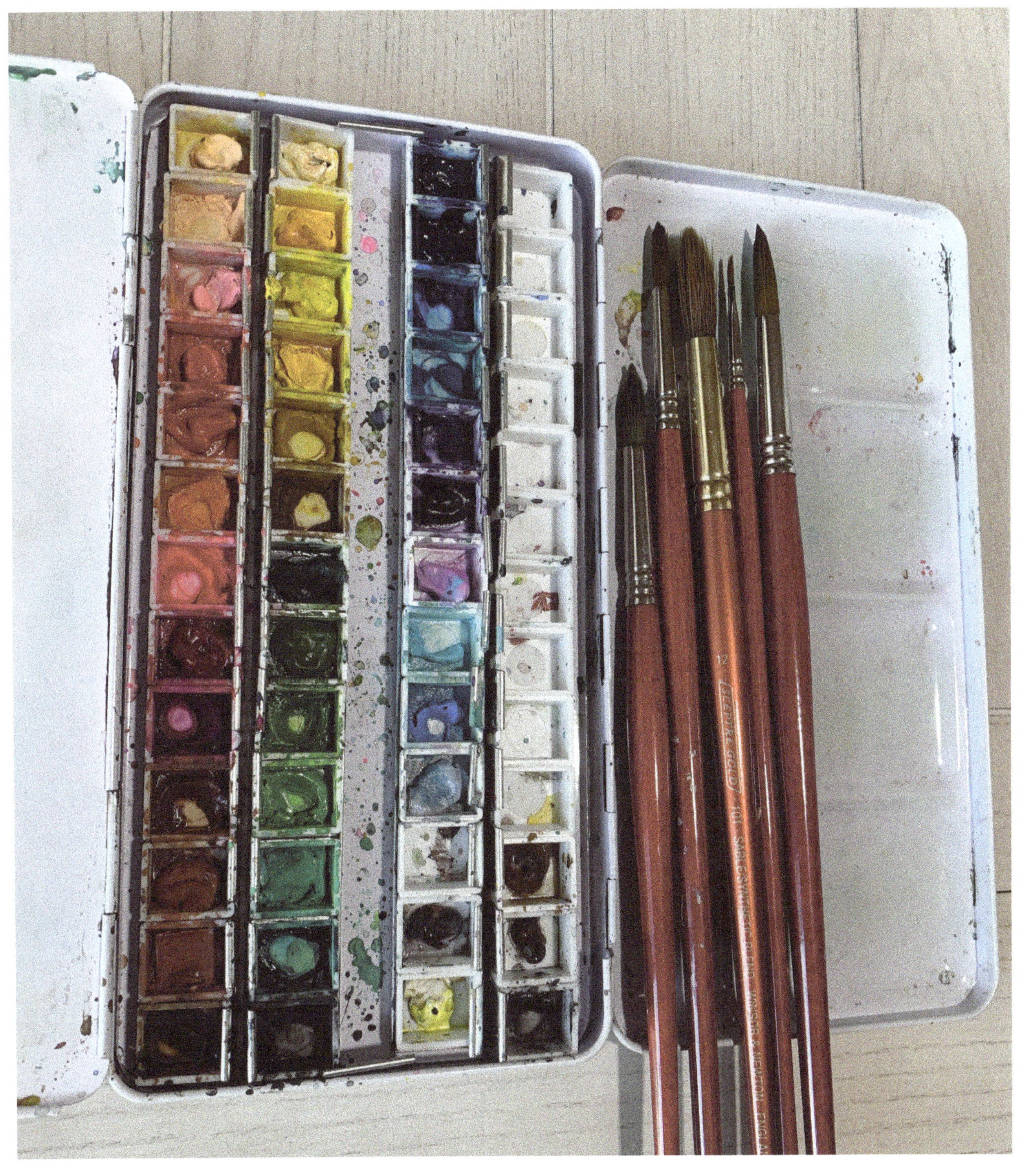

I also love to use brush markers, like Tombow, for my illustrations. They are great for making bold and expressive lines, to enhance your art. In addition, I love artist pens of various thicknesses. They are great if you want to show a higher level of detail in your illustrations.
Also, don't forget some pencils for sketching, as well as an eraser.

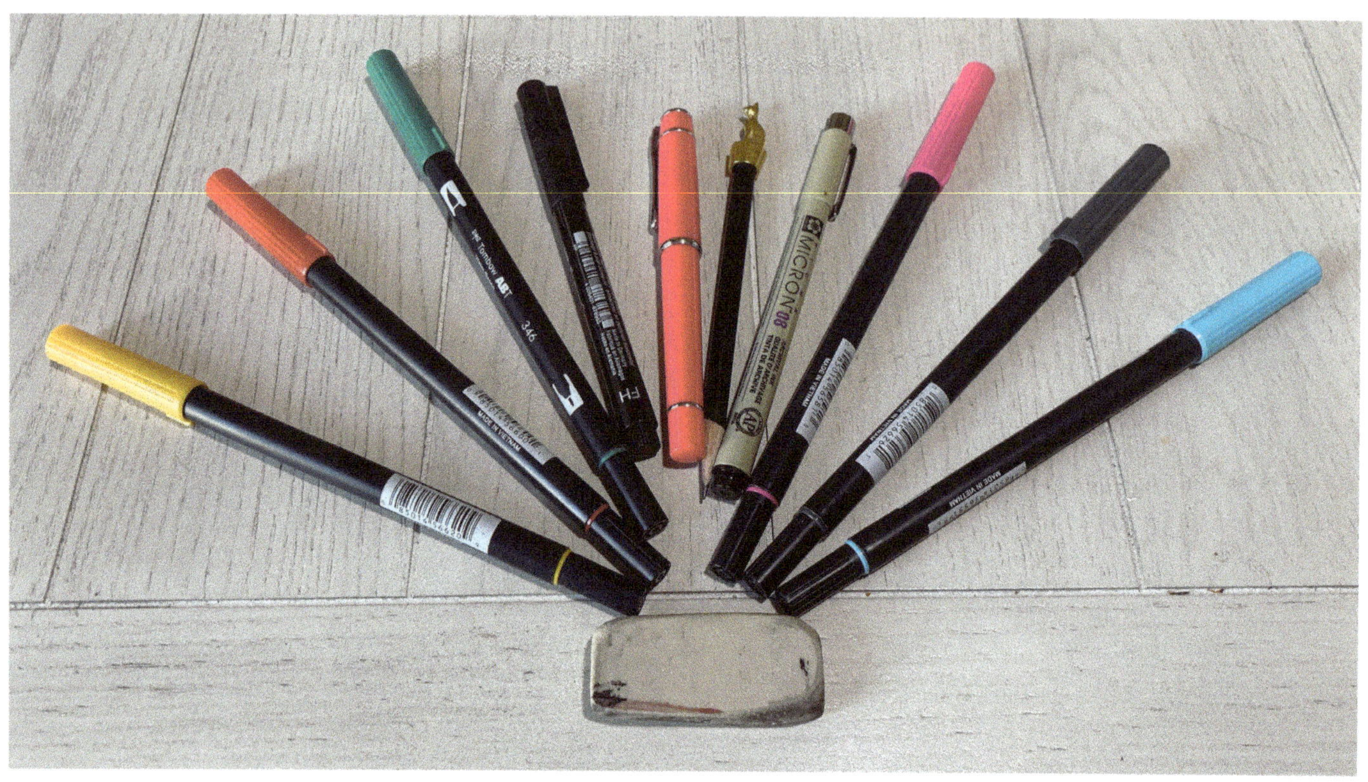

I also recommend getting a portrait pallet marker set. You can play with using these markers to outline your face illustrations, as well as to add shading to the faces.
Finally, you will need a nice pad of your favorite watercolor paper.
I recommend a spiral bound pad, with paper thickness of at least 140 lb.

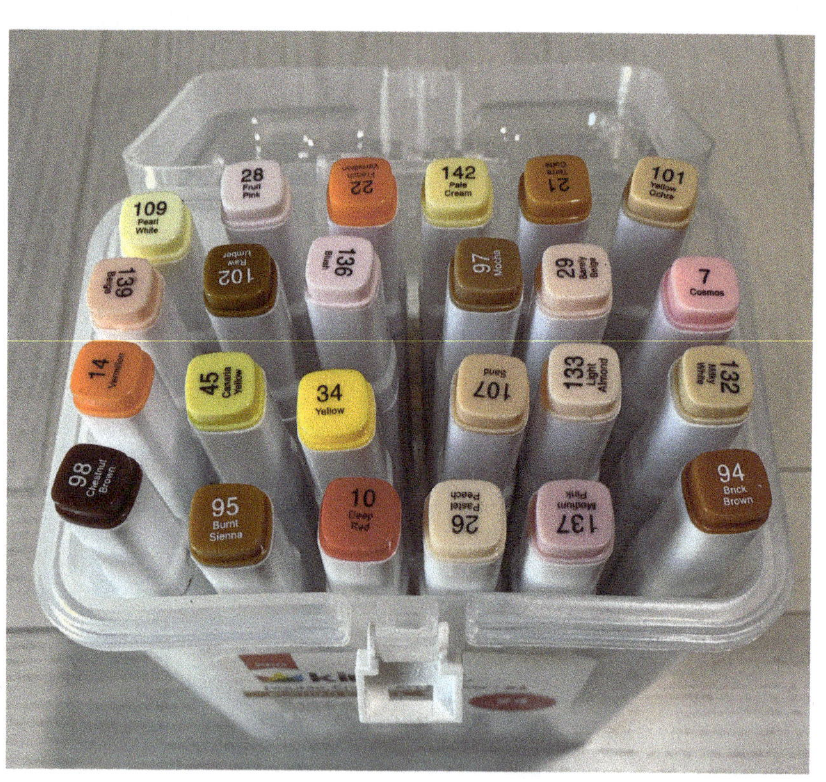

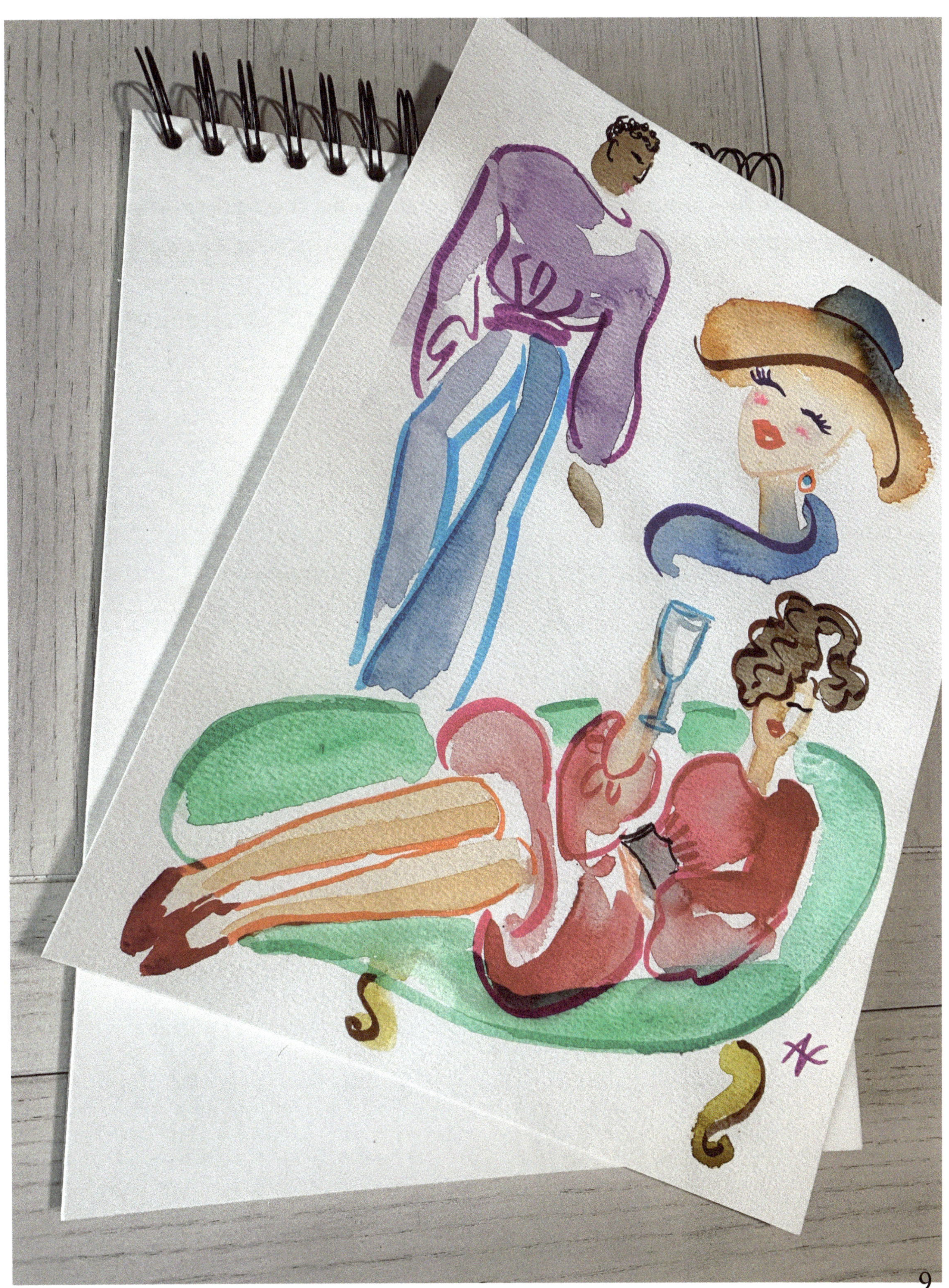

Basic Face Drawings

Let's start by going over the basics of drawing the face. Here are front and side views of a female and male faces. The eyes go at the middle of the head, not at the top. The lips go in between the nose and the bottom of the chin. Tops of the ears generally align up with the corners of the eyes.

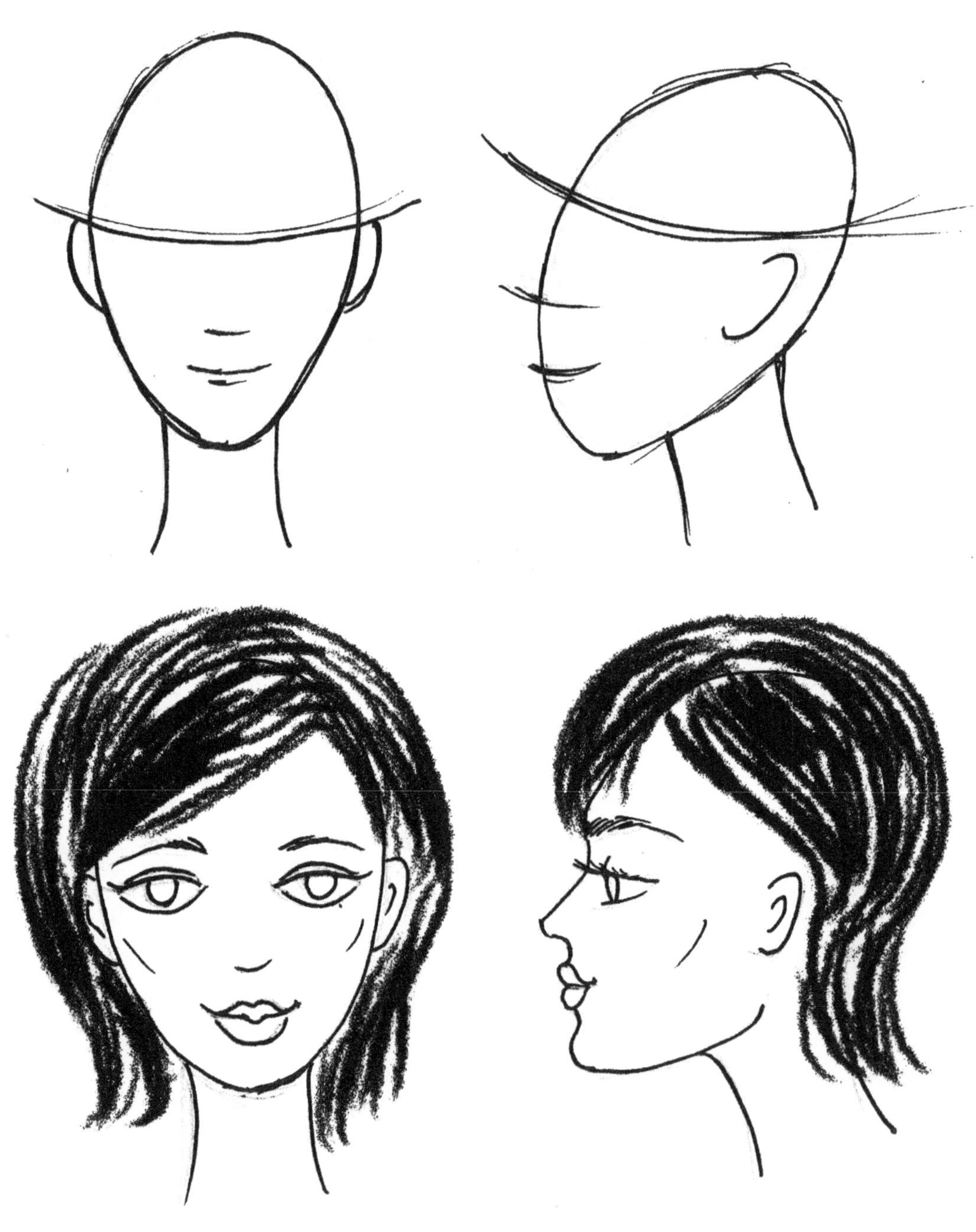

While there are many variations in individuals, female and male faces generally have slightly different proportions and features. Therefore, when we make illustrations, we will emphasize the features that make each gender stand out. For example, men have a wider, and more pronounced jawline, smaller eyes, larger noses, thicker eyebrows, smaller and less noticeable lips/mouth.

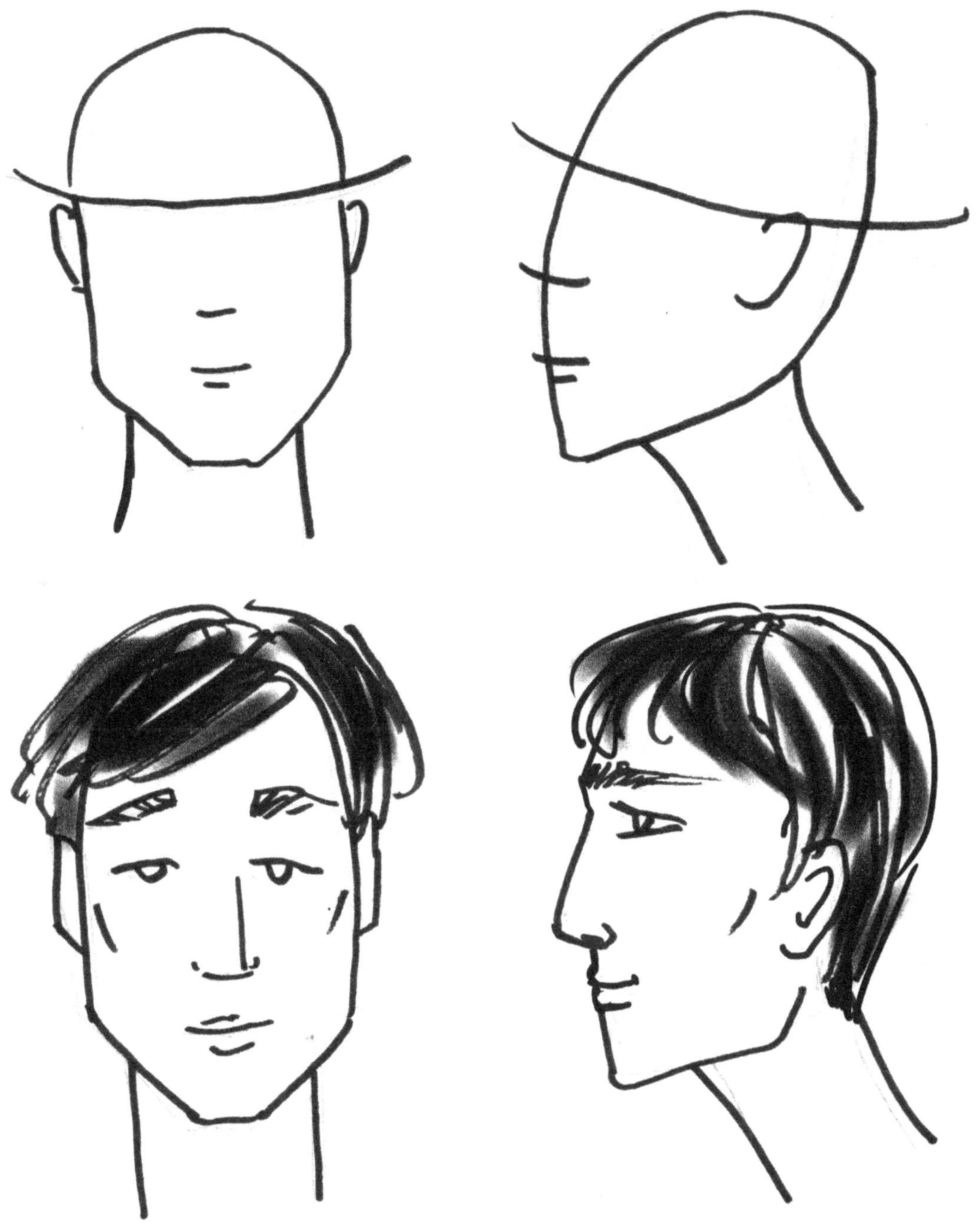

Facial Features

In the next few pages we will go into drawing and painting individual facial features. First we will sketch out different types features, then we will apply a layer of watercolor. Lastly, we will add an outline with our fleshtone markers.
We will start with various nose shapes. Side and front views.
Using a pencil, copy the following

Noses

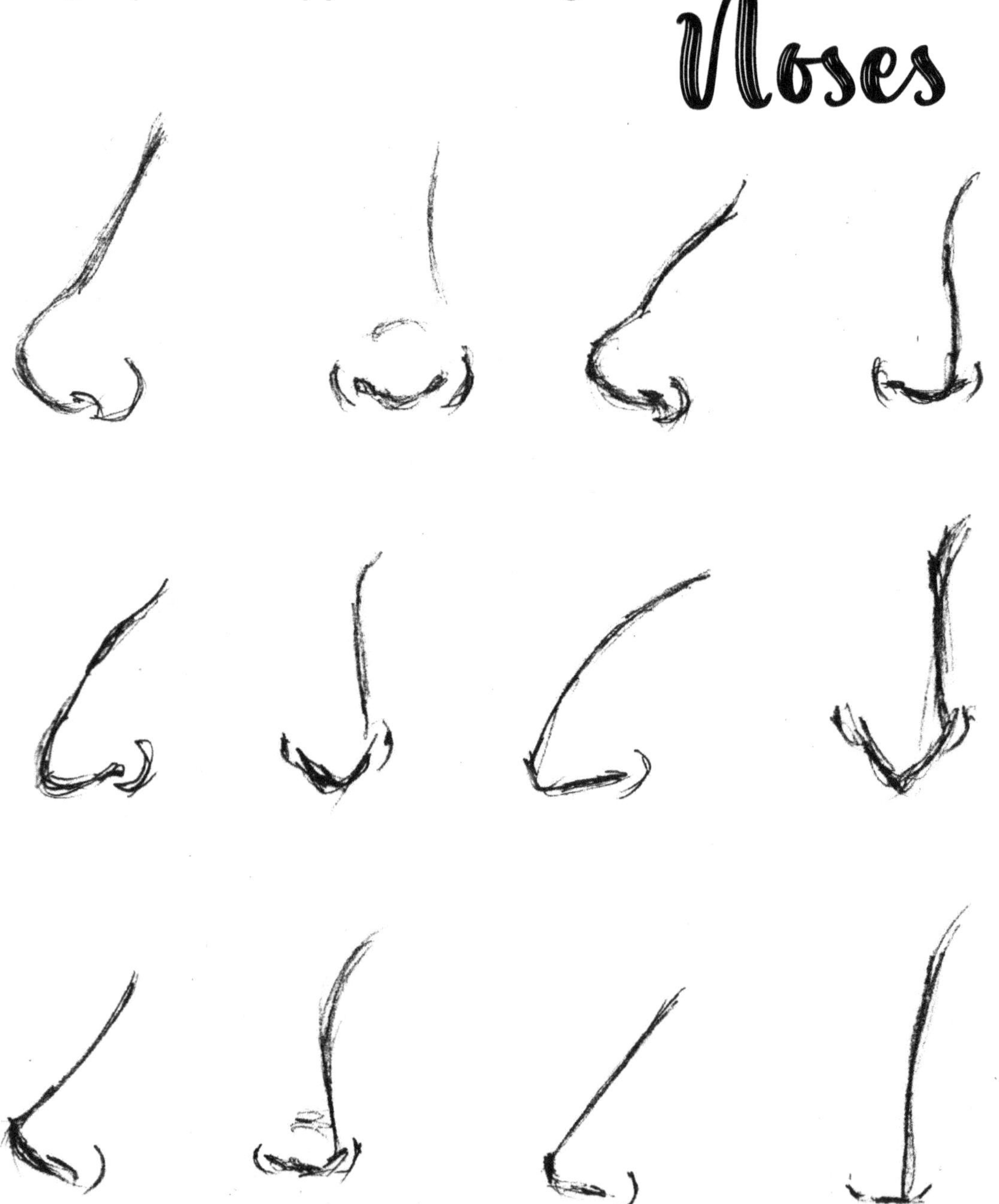

Next step is adding a layer of watercolor. Use the colors from your pallet that would imitate natural human skin tones. Some examples are on the portrait pallet page. Leave some of the areas of the nose white, to show a highlight, such as on the side or tip of the nose.

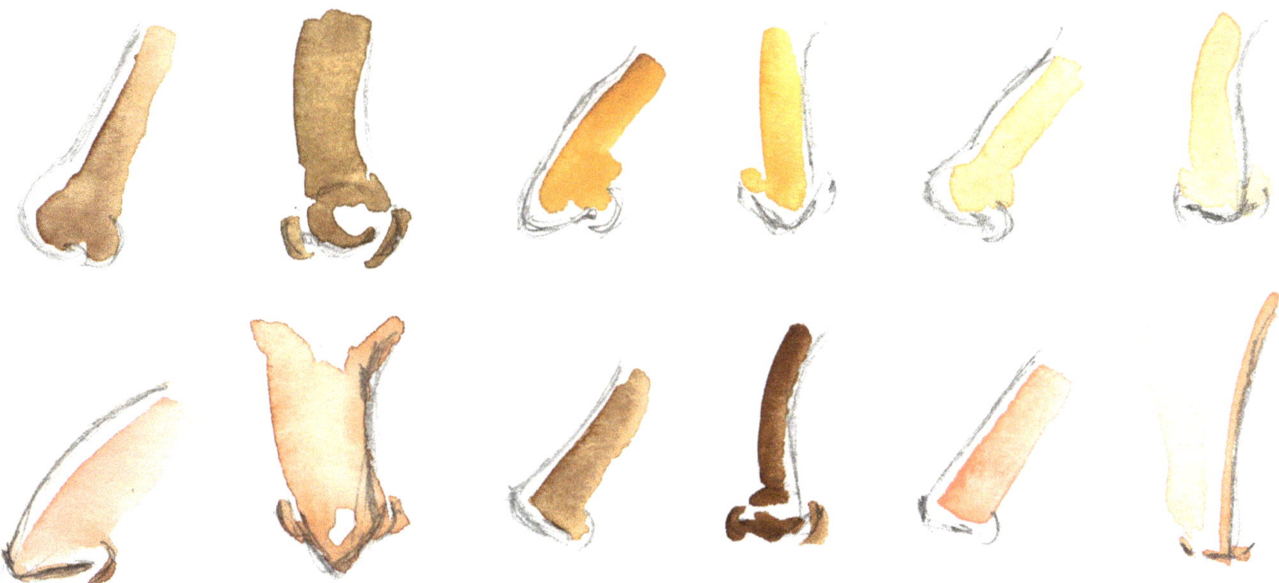

Once the watercolor has dried, you can add outlines to your noses. Using various shades of flesh tone markers, apply thin, playful contours. Indicate nostrils with simple strokes. Do not over-render or add too many details.

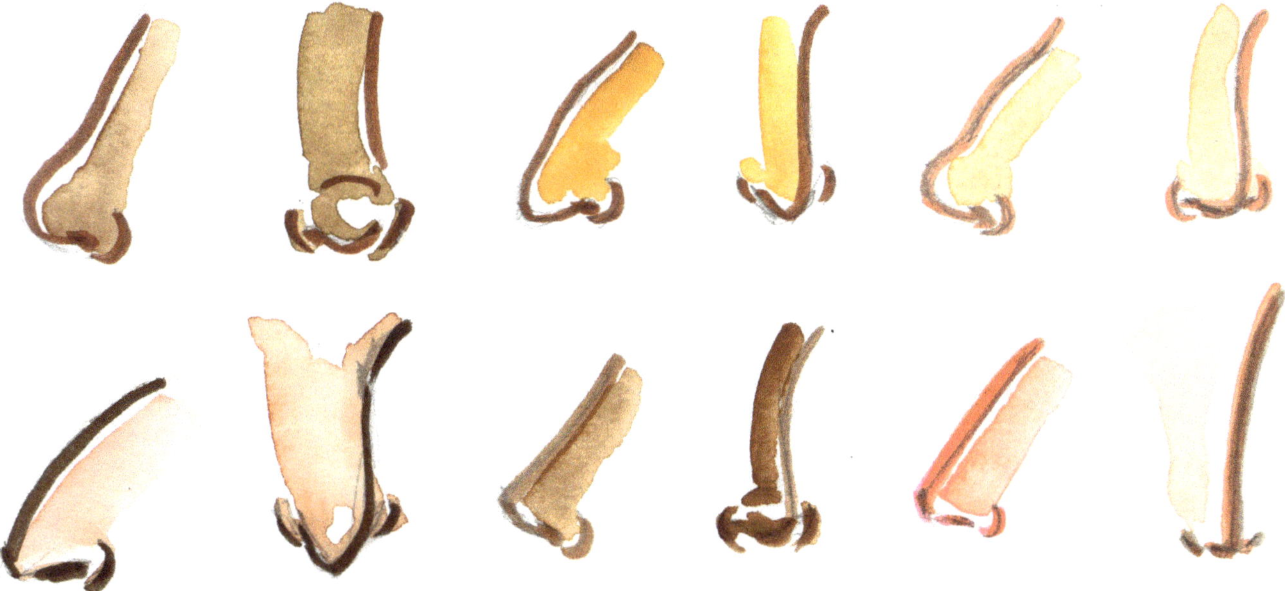

Now let's draw eyes. Here are several different kinds of eye shapes. As well, there is a side view of the eye on the face. Copy the following

Eyes

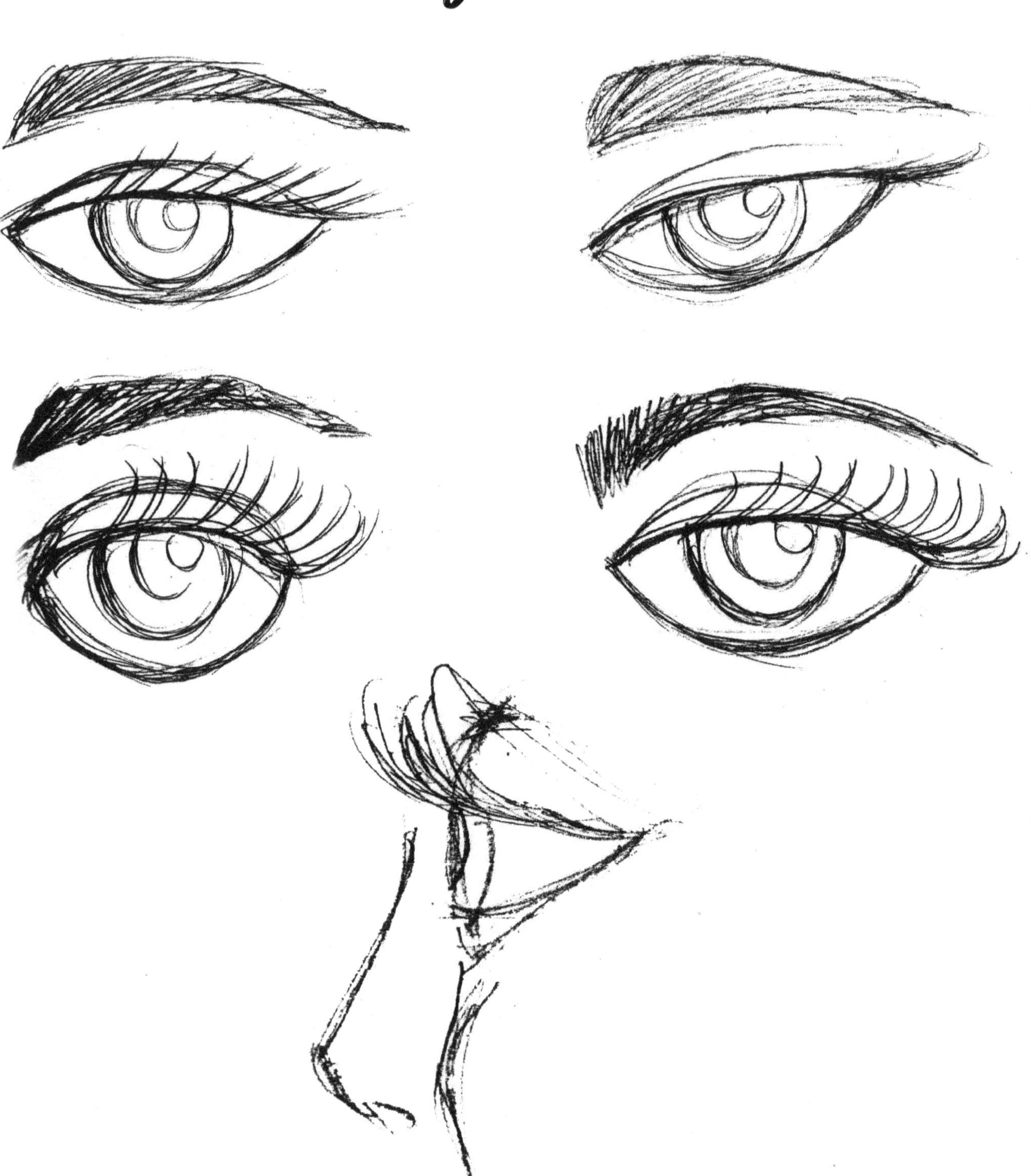

Now let's apply watercolor. Leave the white of the paper
for eye highlights on the pupils, as well as the brow bone.
You can use blue, brown and green watercolors for the
irises. You can also indicate the roundness of the eyeballs
by applying slight shading at the corners of the eyes.

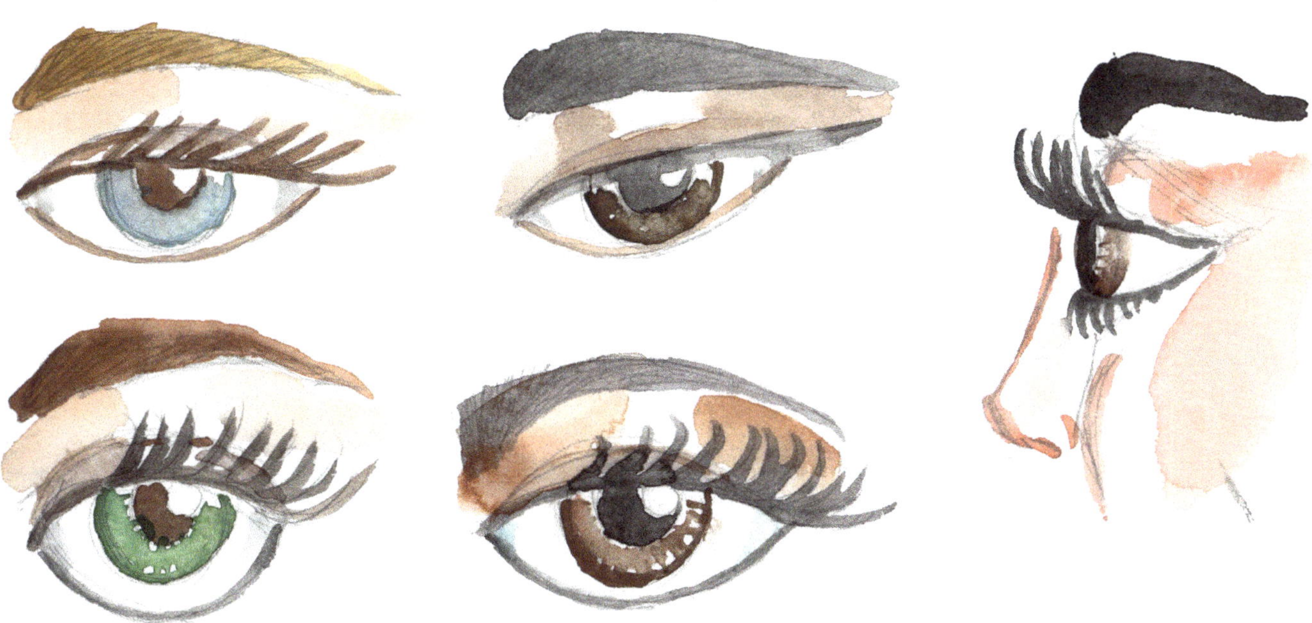

After the watercolor dries, you can apply marker details,
as shown. You can indicate hair on the eyebrows, eyelashes,
accents on the irises, and outlines on the face and eyes.

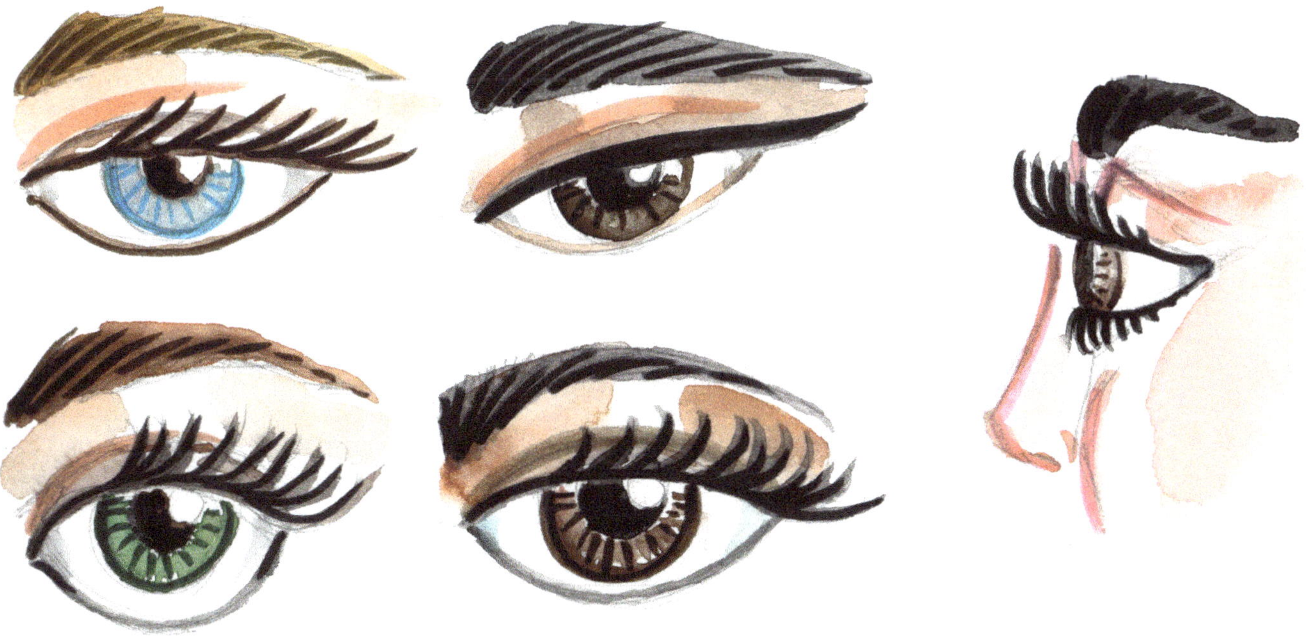

Now let's practice drawing lips. Lips also come in many shapes and sizes. The upper lip is generally a bit thinner than the lower lip, but not always. You can indicate a slight smile by drawing tiny dashes at the corners of the lips.
Practice drawing the following *Lips*

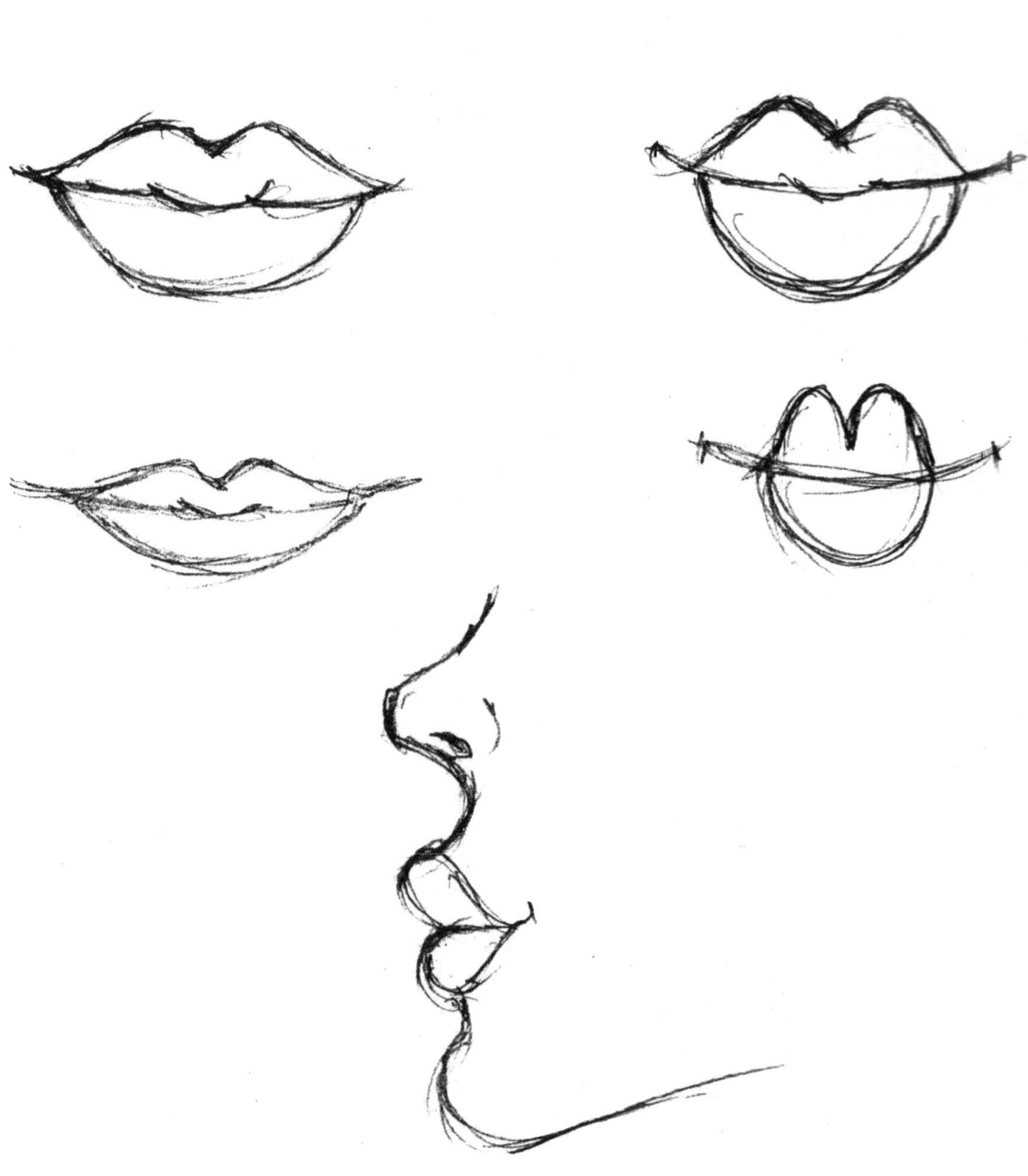

Apply your watercolors. Use reds, pinks and reddish-purple shades. Leave the white of the paper for the highlight on the lower lip.

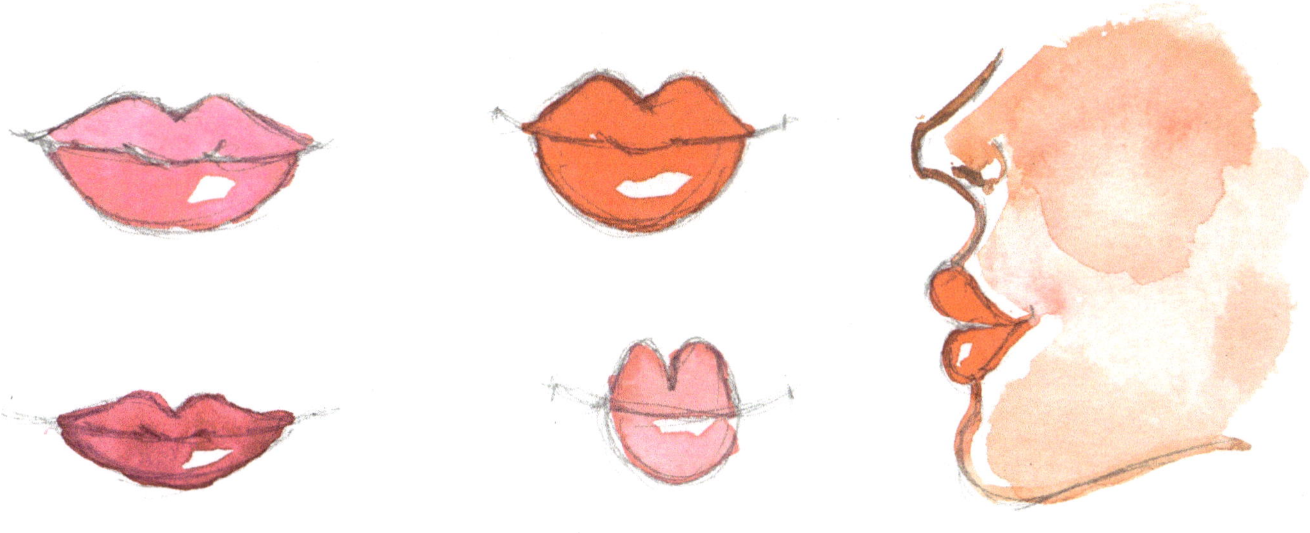

After the watercolor has dried, use markers to add outlines to the lips/side view of the face/lips. Try to match the markers to the watercolor, but use a darker shade.

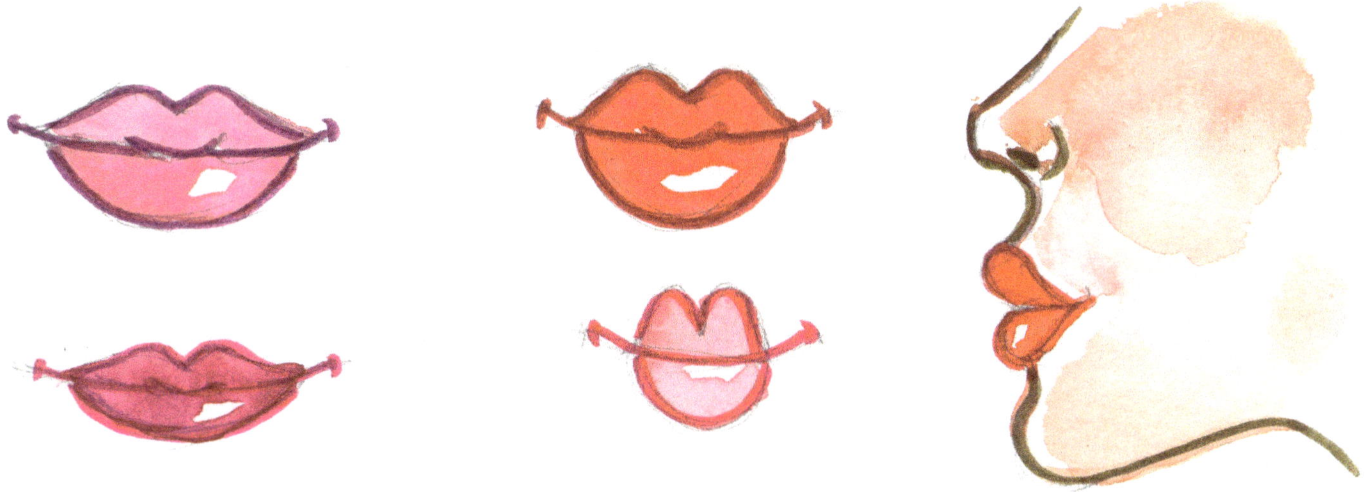

Portrait Pallet Colors

Here are suggested colors to use for your watercolor face illustrations. However, you can use your own versions that come with the watercolor set of your choosing.

Some of the colors shown here are: yellow ocre, white, jaulle brilliant, red ocre, brown, permanent yellow deep, raw umber, brown red, Vandyke brown, opera. Color names may vary by set. You can use colors as is or you can layer colors and dilute them with water for a lighter appearance, and you can also mix different colors. I encourage you to experiment and see what results you can achieve.

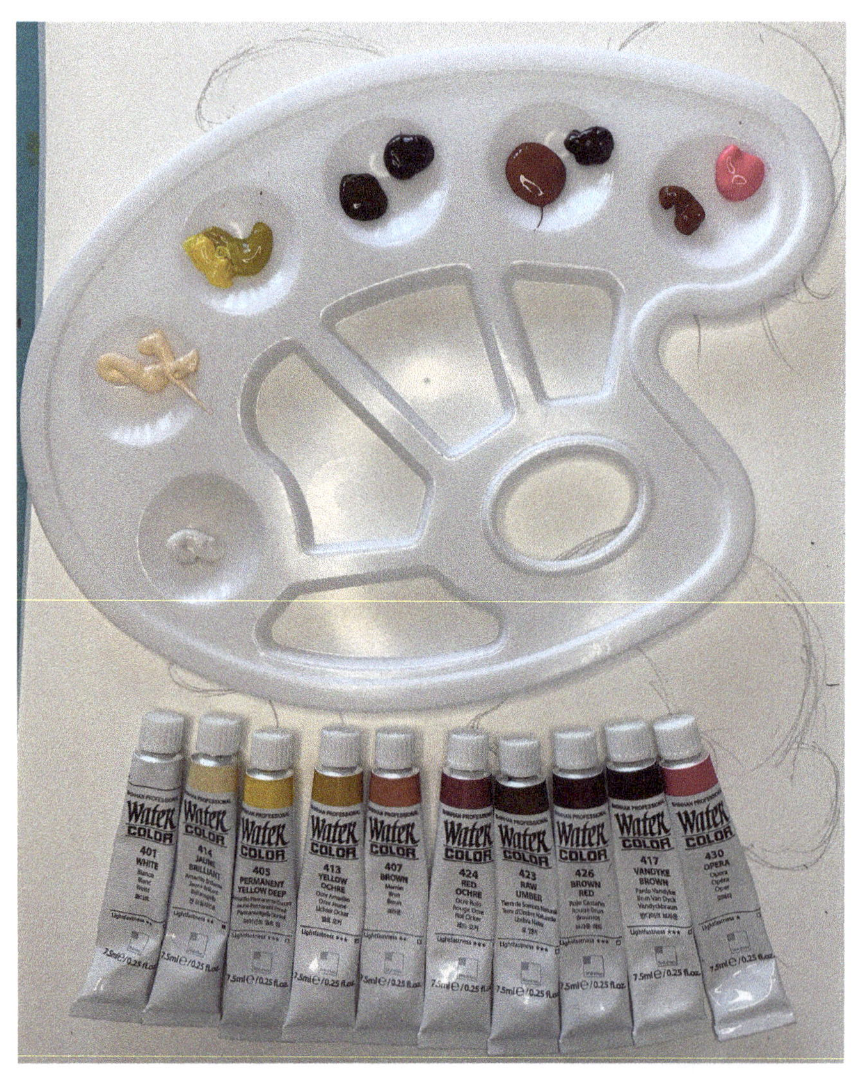

These are stylized simple profile face drawings showing the various colors you can use.

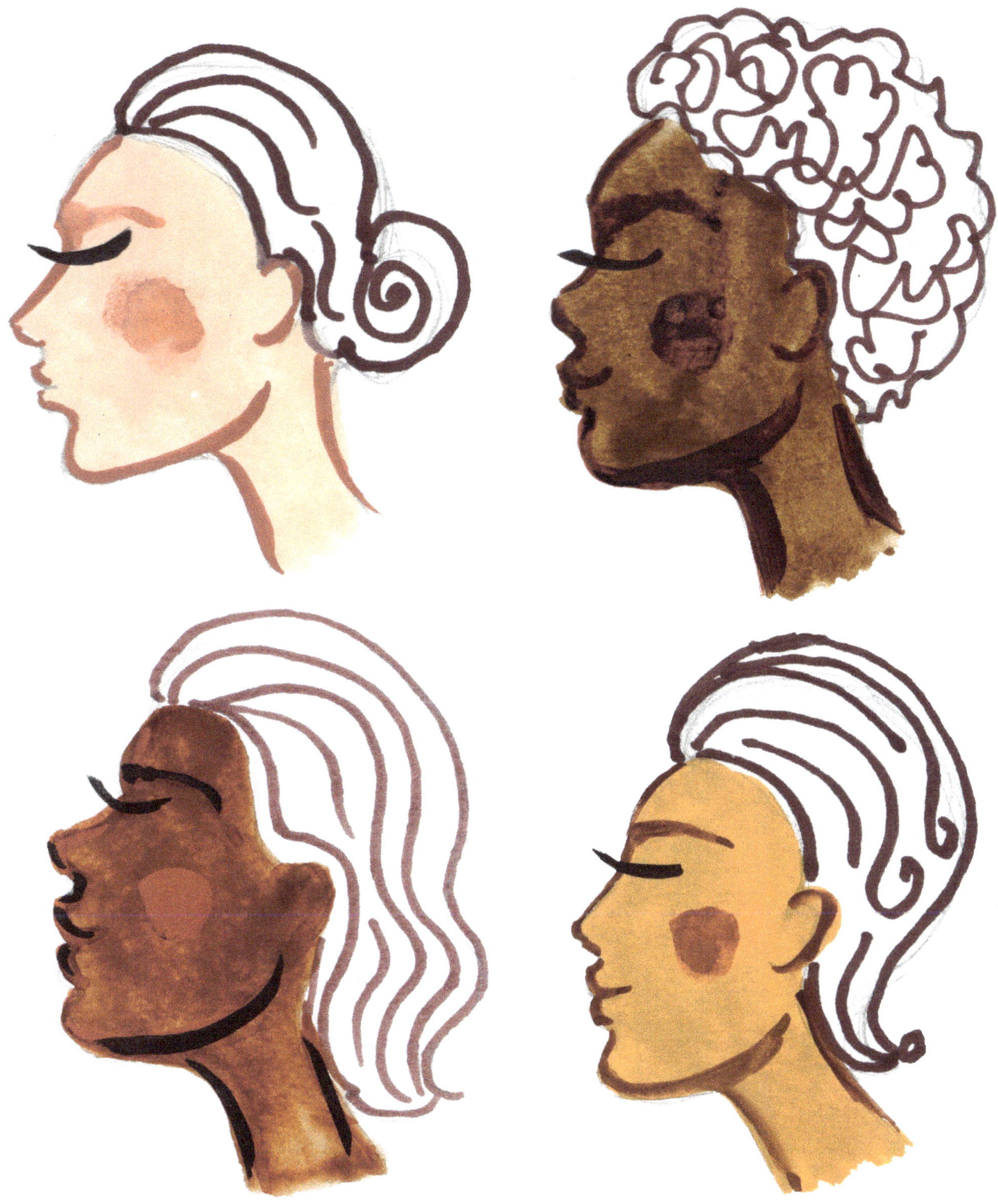

You can also use markers once you apply your watercolors. You can add outlines to your paintings, as well as partially draw parts of the portraits in markers.

Use flesh tone markers that are darker than your base face color for outlines and to indicate shading. You can also use darker paint shades and a thin brush for this purpose.

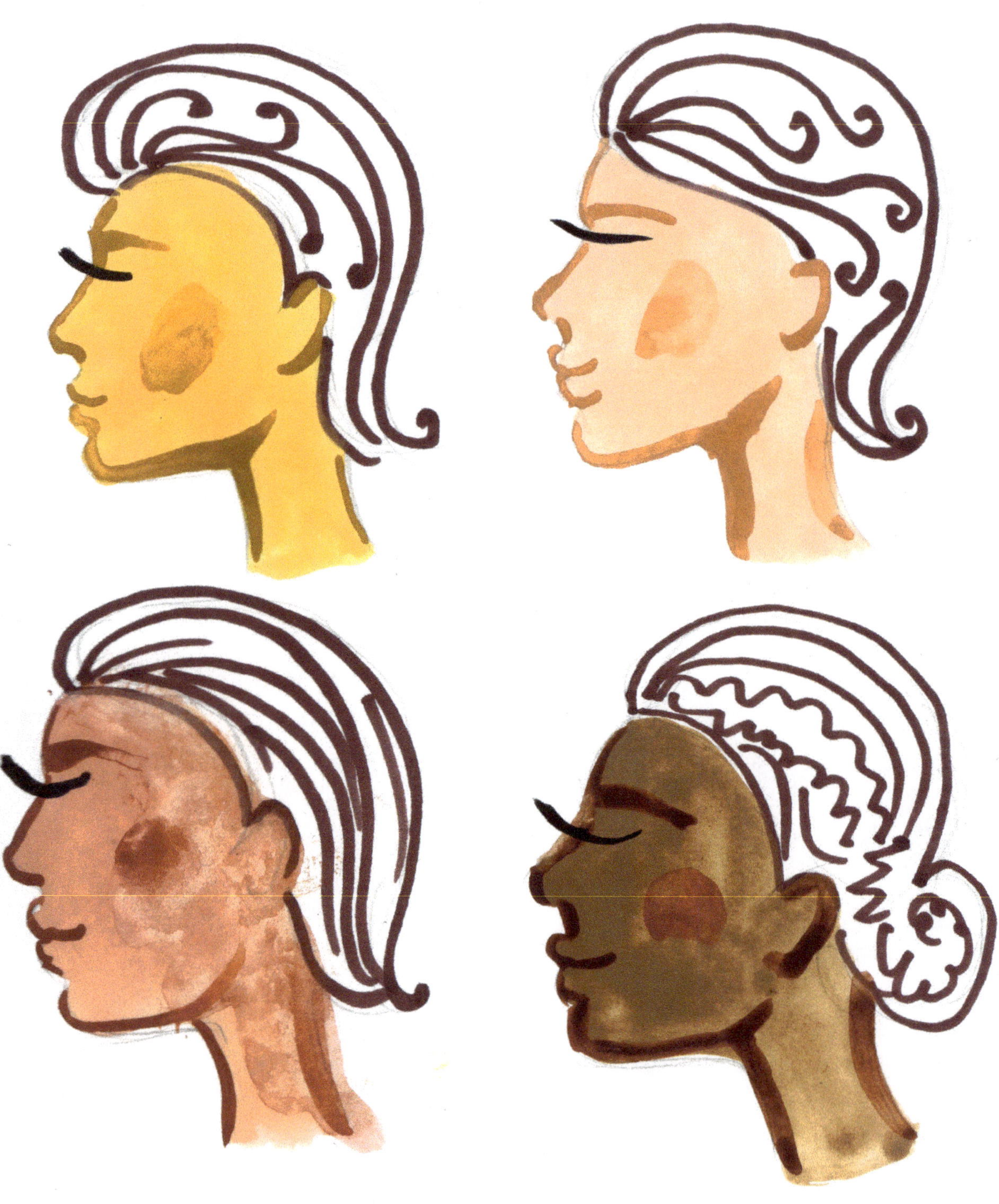

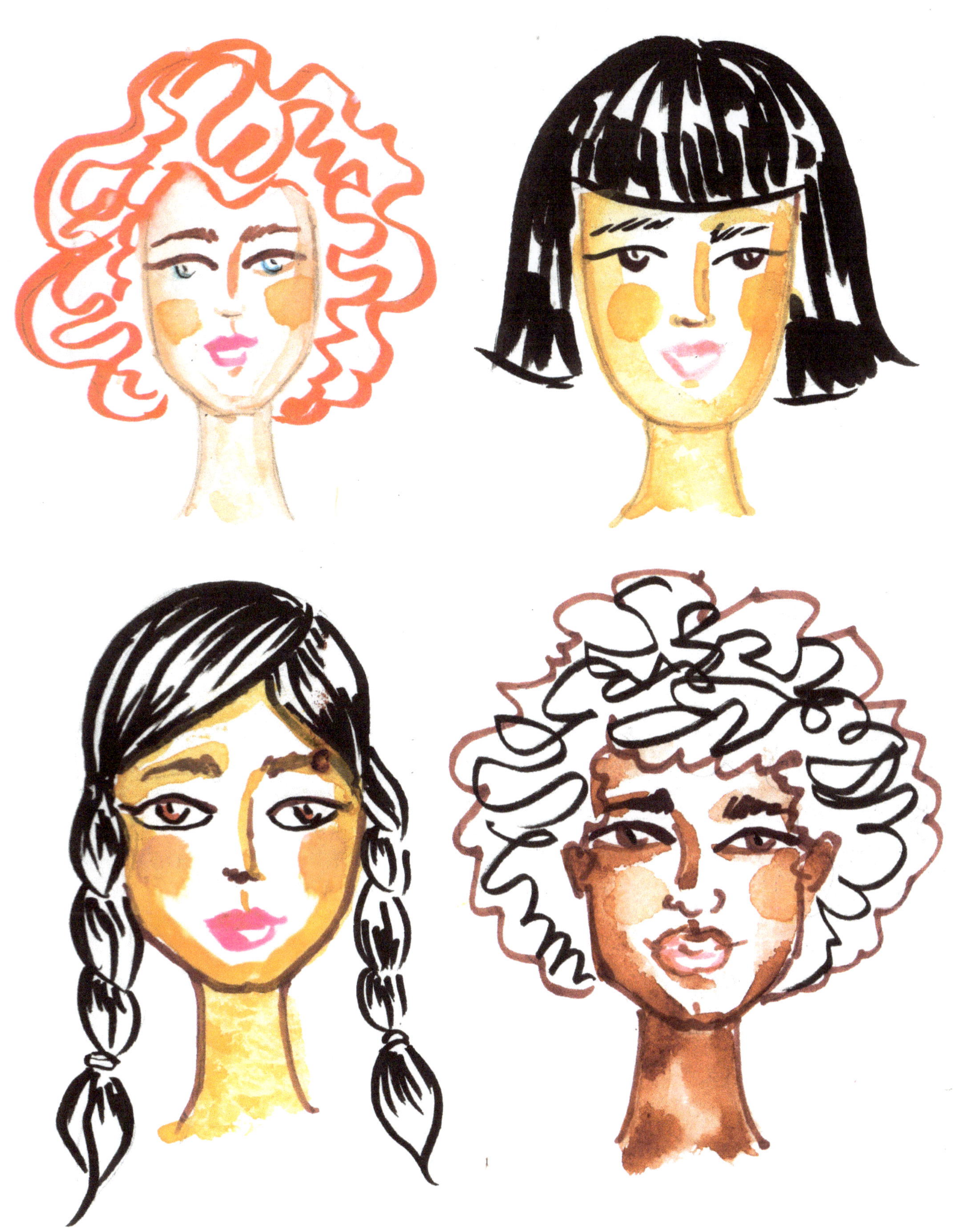

Use the white of the paper to give dimension and light up your watercolor face illustrations.

Making Blends & Gradients

Let us practice making watercolor blends. You can blend different colors - complimentary colors, cool or warm colors, or shades of the same color, fading from saturated to less saturated.

First draw out basic head shape silhouettes, then play with painting within each, as you see in these examples.

You can paint using various techniques. Options include, first wetting the paper and then painting on the wet paper, or simply painting directly on dry paper with a wet paintbrush. Make sure your brush has plenty of water, choose a color on your pallet and swoosh the brush with the color.

Once the brush has enough color and not too much water, paint in your shapes. You can get very creative with the colors you choose and the way you apply the color.

Dab off excess water from the brush or paper with a tissue. You may also use a wet brush to correct any imperfections in your paintings.

In the examples below, you can see that there are many ways of blending watercolors together. You can create many interesting gradient combinations and feathering effects. Use more or less water and experiment, to see what results you achieve. The more you try, the more confident you will get combining watercolors.

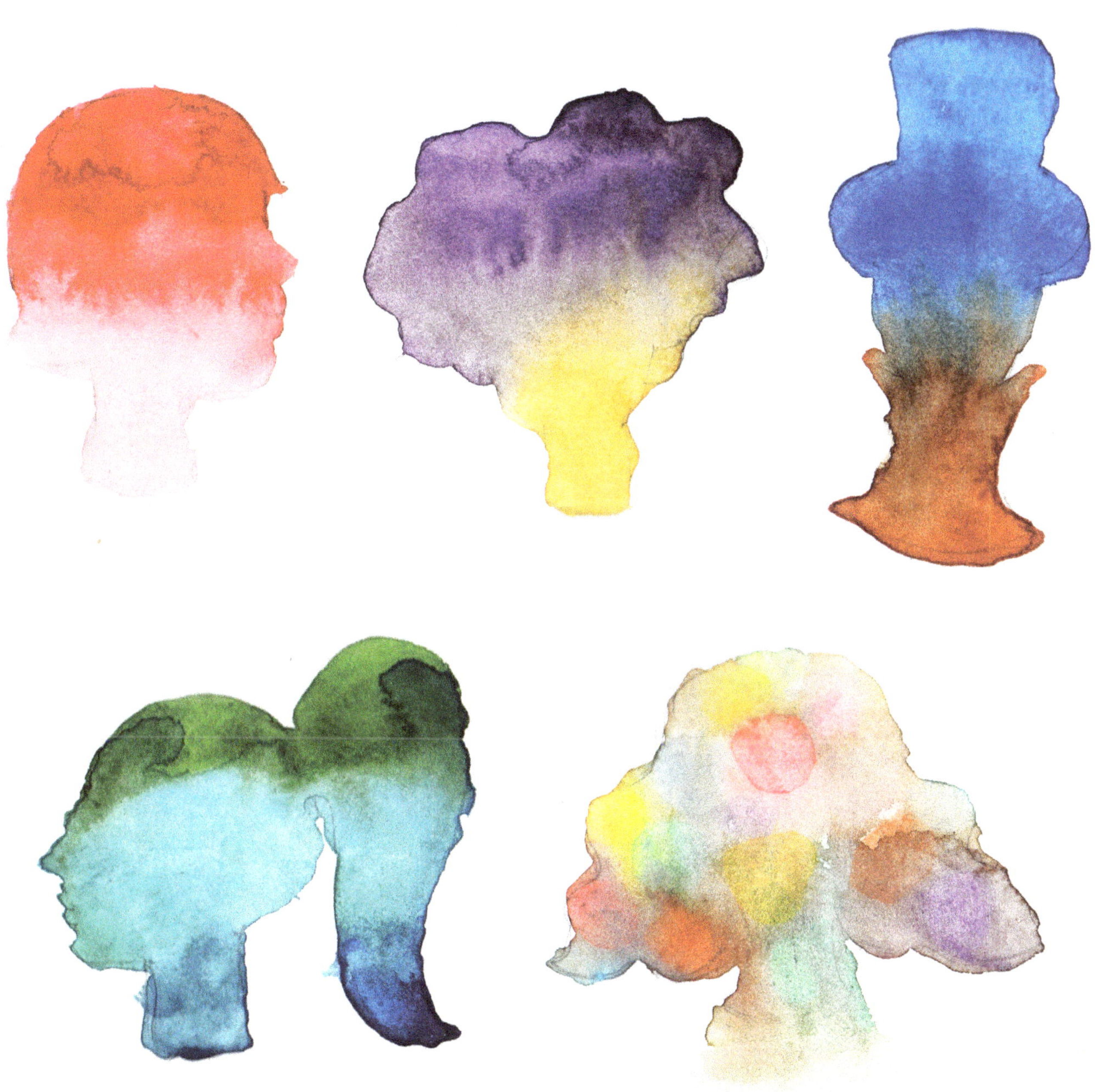

Layering Colors To Create Shadows

We can add shading to our faces by layering darker shades of our main color and creating color blends with water.

First paint the shape, then let it dry fully. After our shape has dried, we can use a darker shade in similar color scheme and add the color on the side you wish the shadow to fall.

Follow the shape as you paint. You can see example swatches of color under each monochromatic shape.

You can achieve darker shades by mixing colors, or by using the colors that come in your watercolor set.

There are various techniques and rules for creating realistic shading on objects. By trying out various paint mixes, you can experiment to achieve your desired painting effects. Rather than focusing on hyper realism, I want you to have fun!

Remember, watercolor is a transparent medium, it is supposed to look fresh, not muddy or over-worked. So, make your faces with the same in mind - fresh, fun, and vibrant!

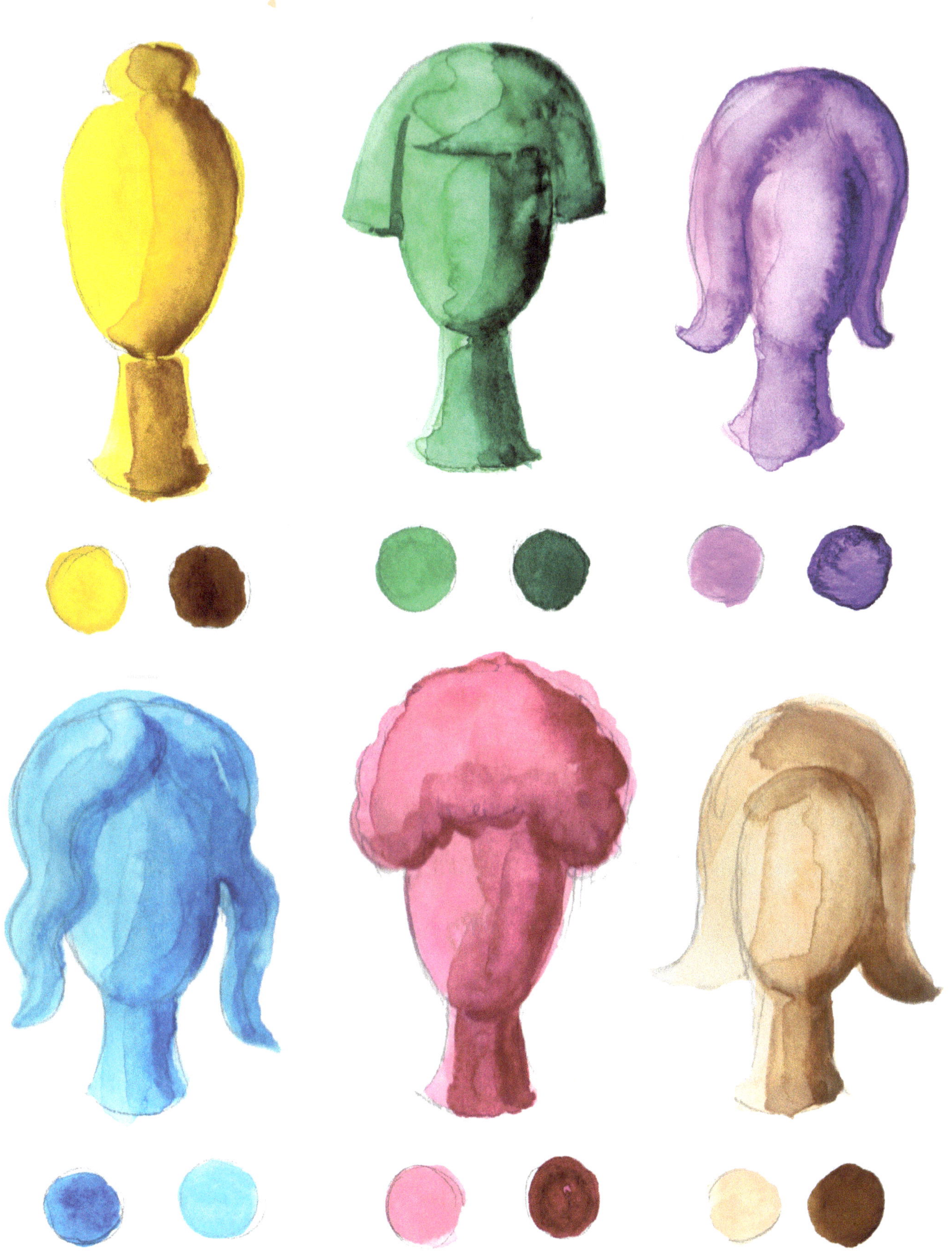

Face Illustrations – Front and Side View

Step 1

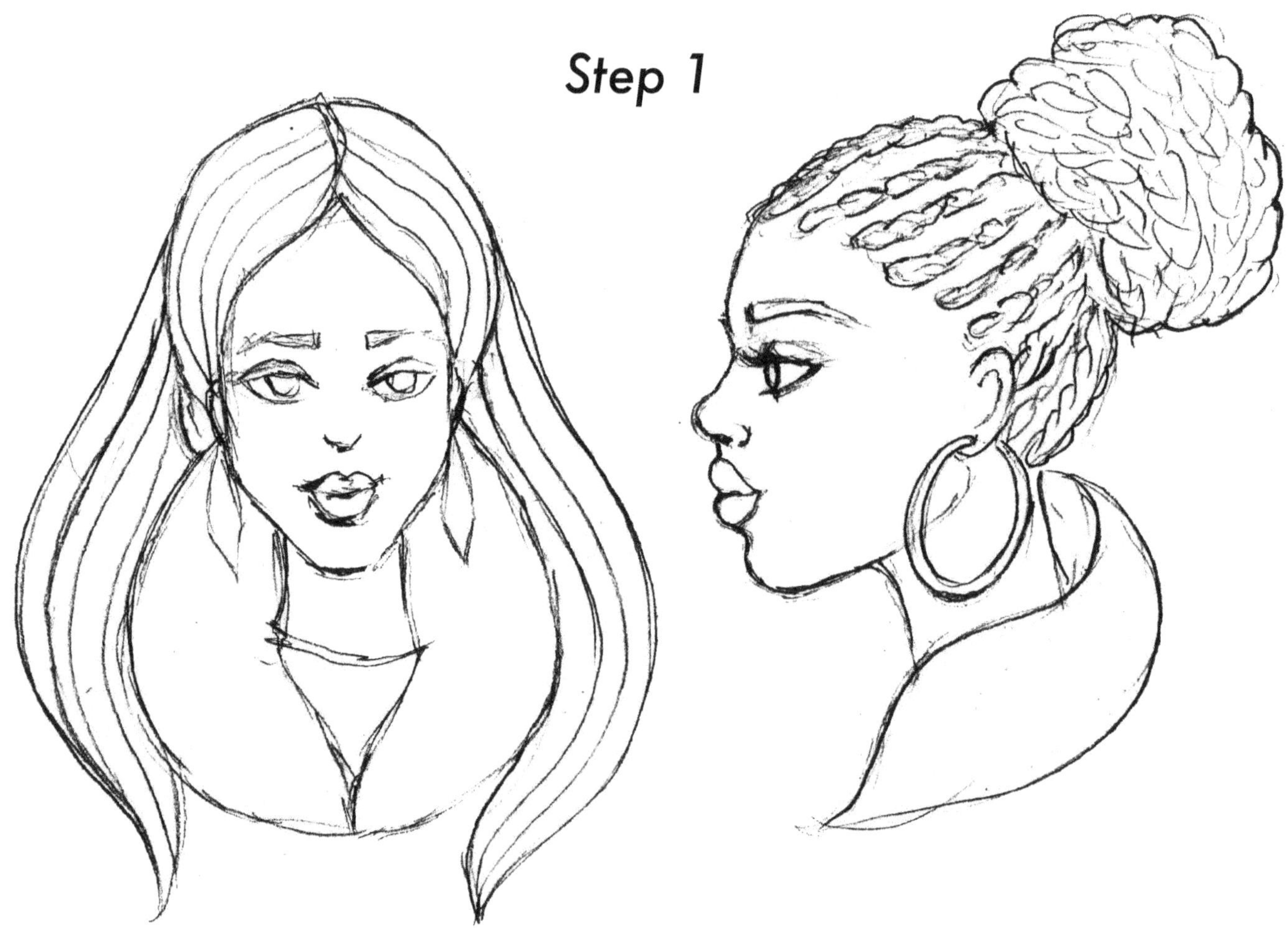

For our first face illustration exercise, we will copy the images above. Use a pencil to sketch out the faces. Pay attention to hair texture and facial proportions. When you draw straight or wavy hair, make it follow, strand by strand, the natural growth pattern and shape of the head. When you draw tightly curly or braided hair, you should indicate the intricate texture of the hair within the strands.

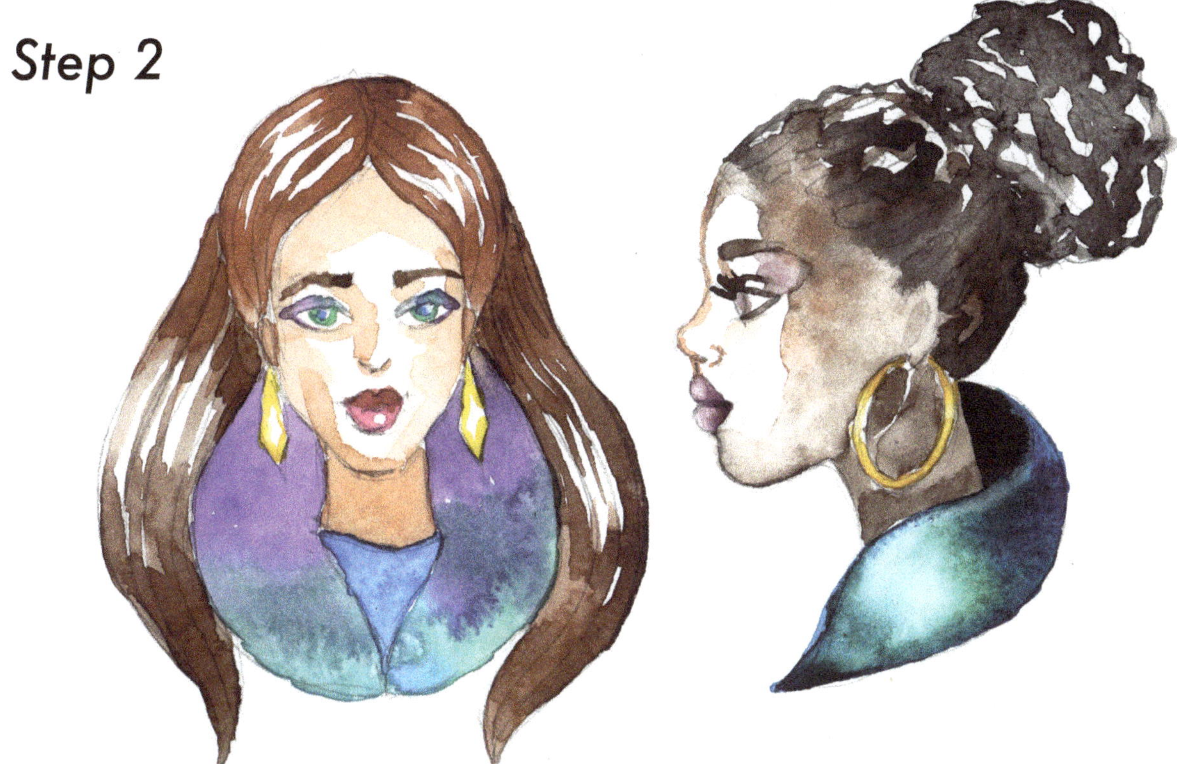

Apply the first layer of watercolor. Leave the white of the paper for highlights. You can let colors run into one another for a beautiful gradient effect.

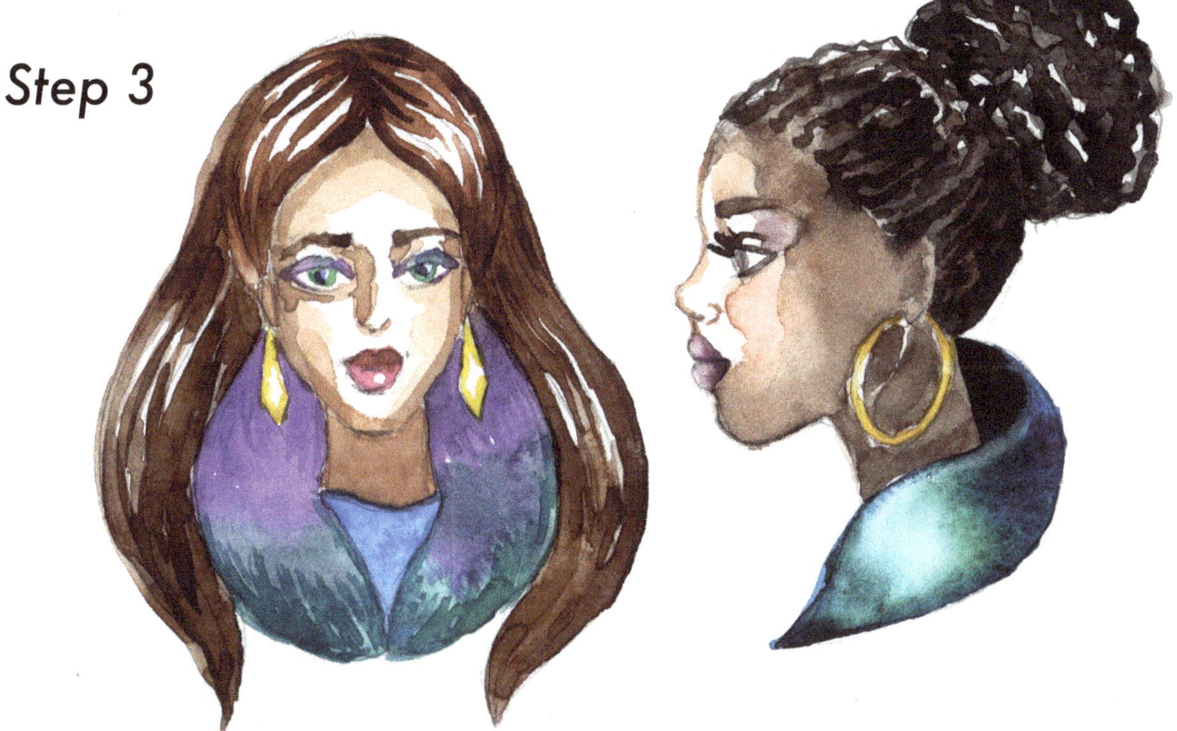

Once the first layer dries, you can apply an additional layer of color. Add more shading by using darker shades of a given color. Add some cheek color, as well as shading in cheeks and nose.

Illustrating Men's Faces

Step 1

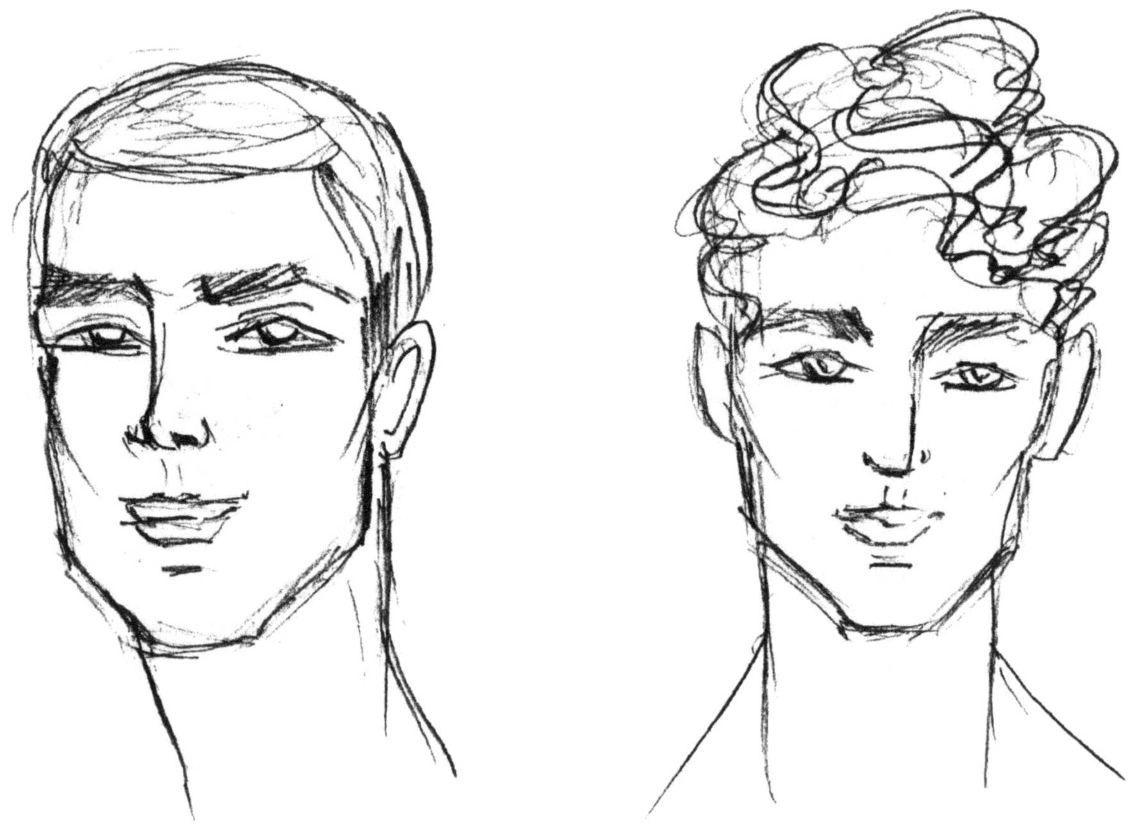

Here we will briefly touch on illustrating men's faces in watercolor. Sketch out these faces in pencil. Pay attention to the way men have more angular jaws, wider necks, smaller eyes and lips. The eyebrows are thicker and wider.

Step 2

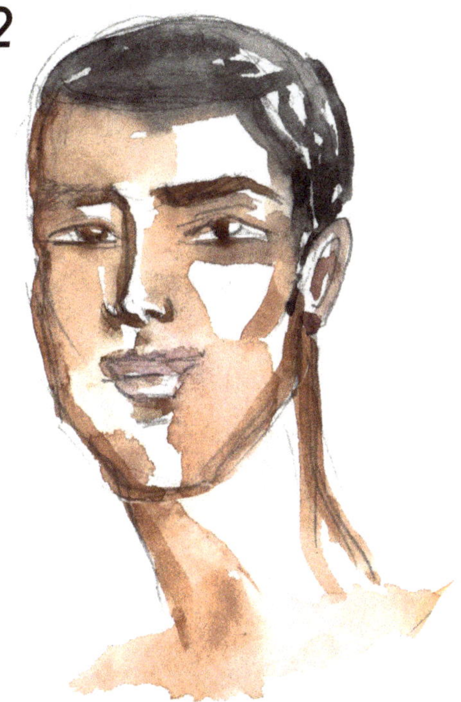 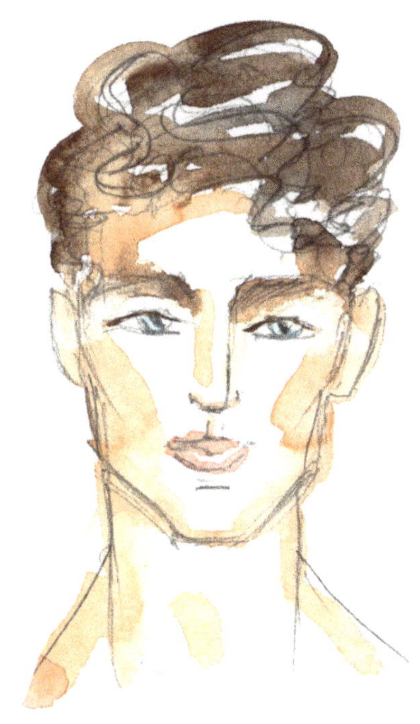

Apply the first layer of watercolor. Leave the white of the paper for highlights. Play with the hair texture, by making playful lines (as you see in the curly haired man.)

Step 3

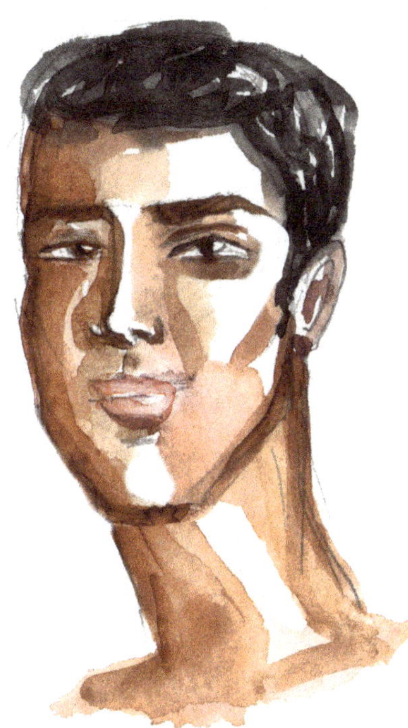 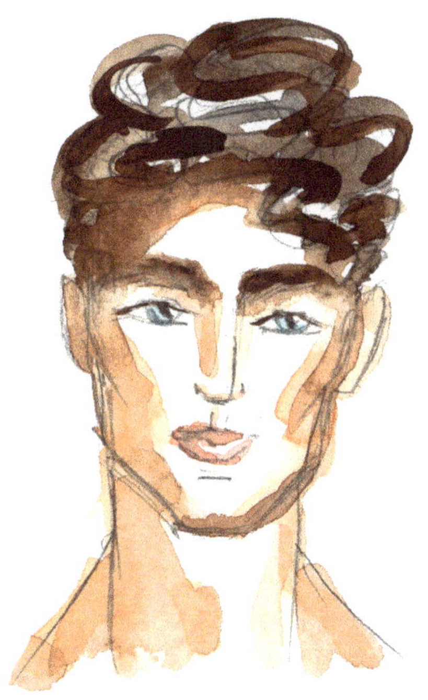

Once the first layer dries, you can apply an additional layer of color. Add more shading by using darker shades of a given color. Add some cheek color, as well as shading in cheeks and nose.

Eyes

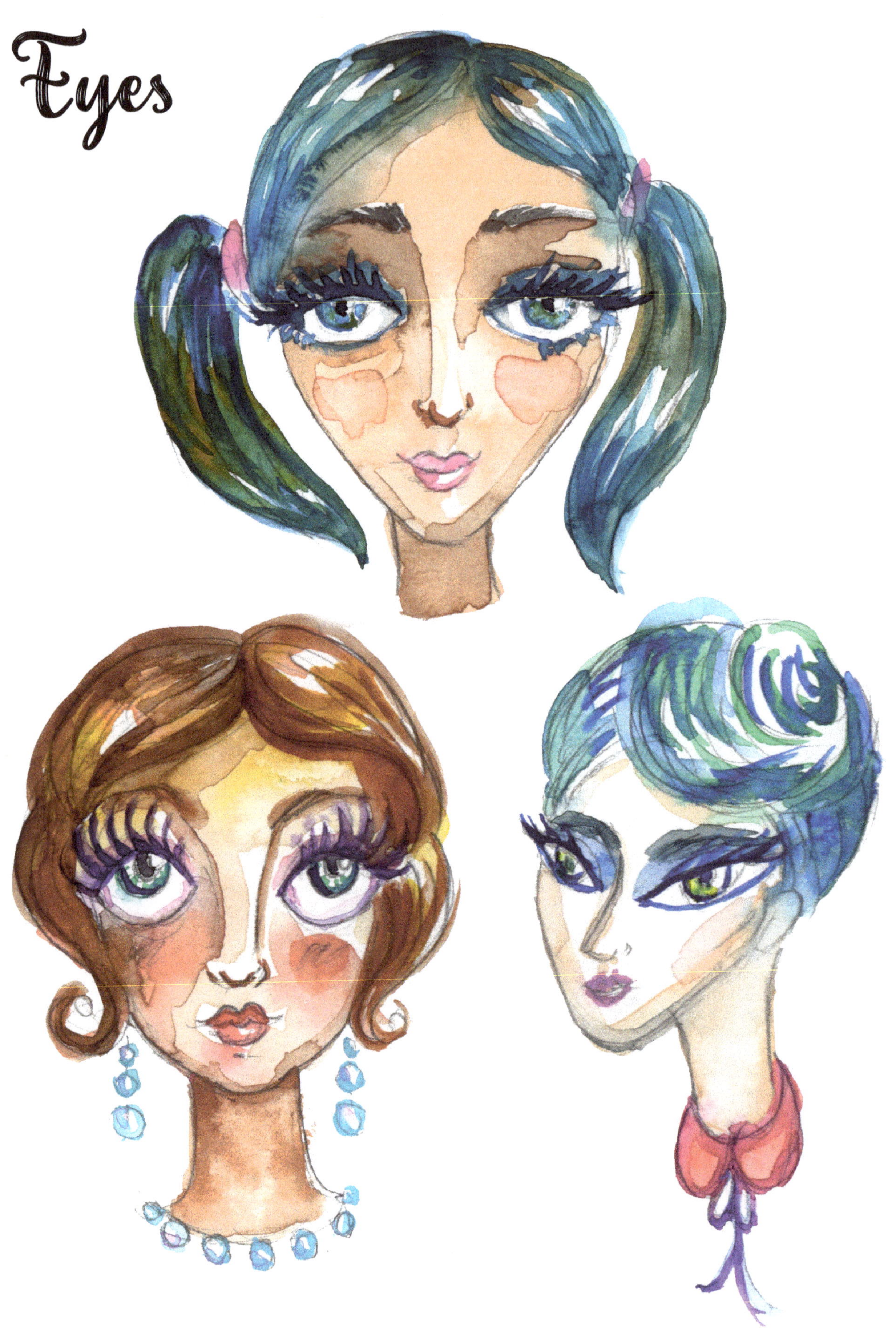

Exaggerating Features

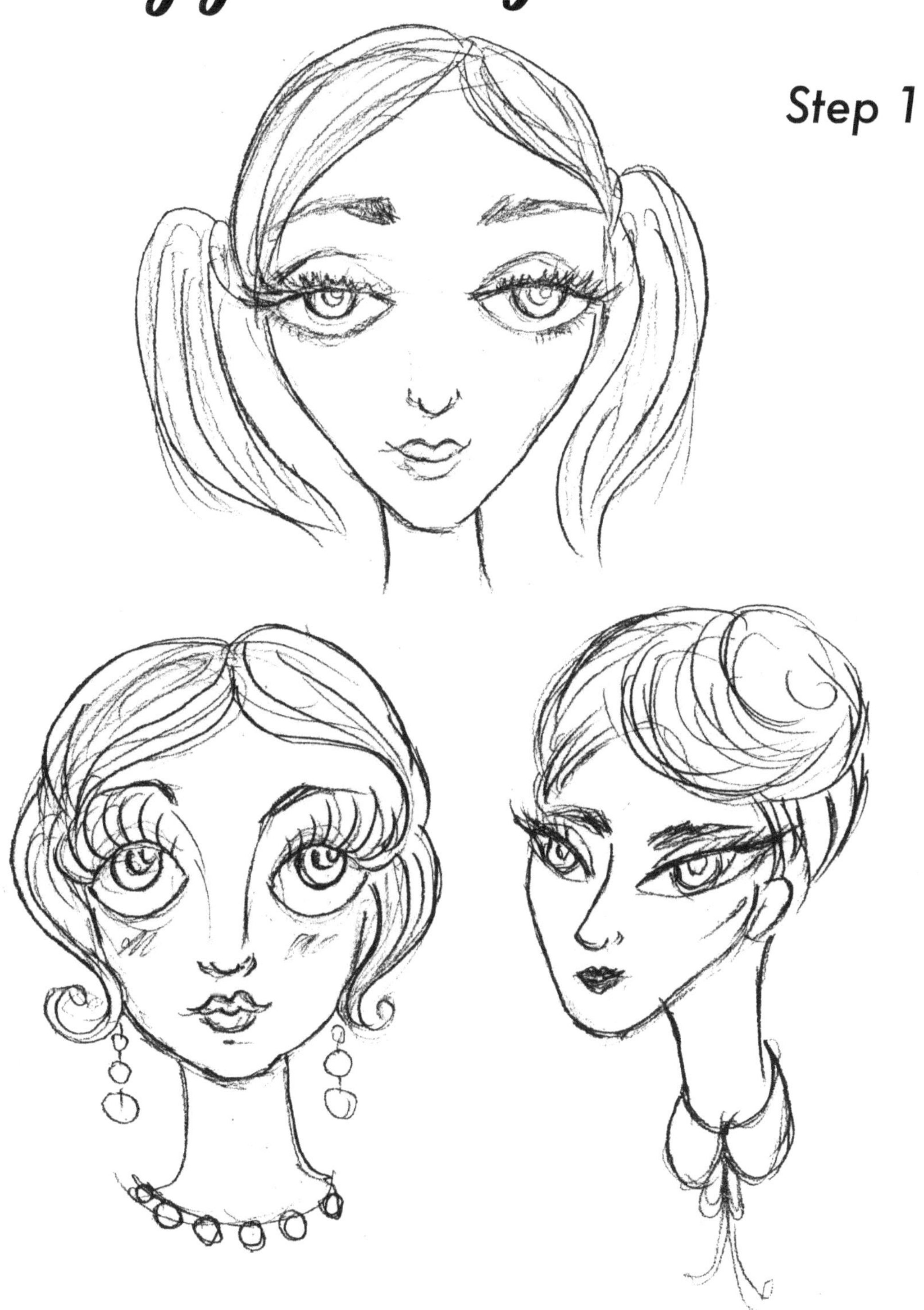

In the next few pages, let's create illustrations that emphasize various features of the face. Such as, eyes, noses and lips. Let's copy these faces. When sketching them, note how the eyes are more prominent than the other facial features.

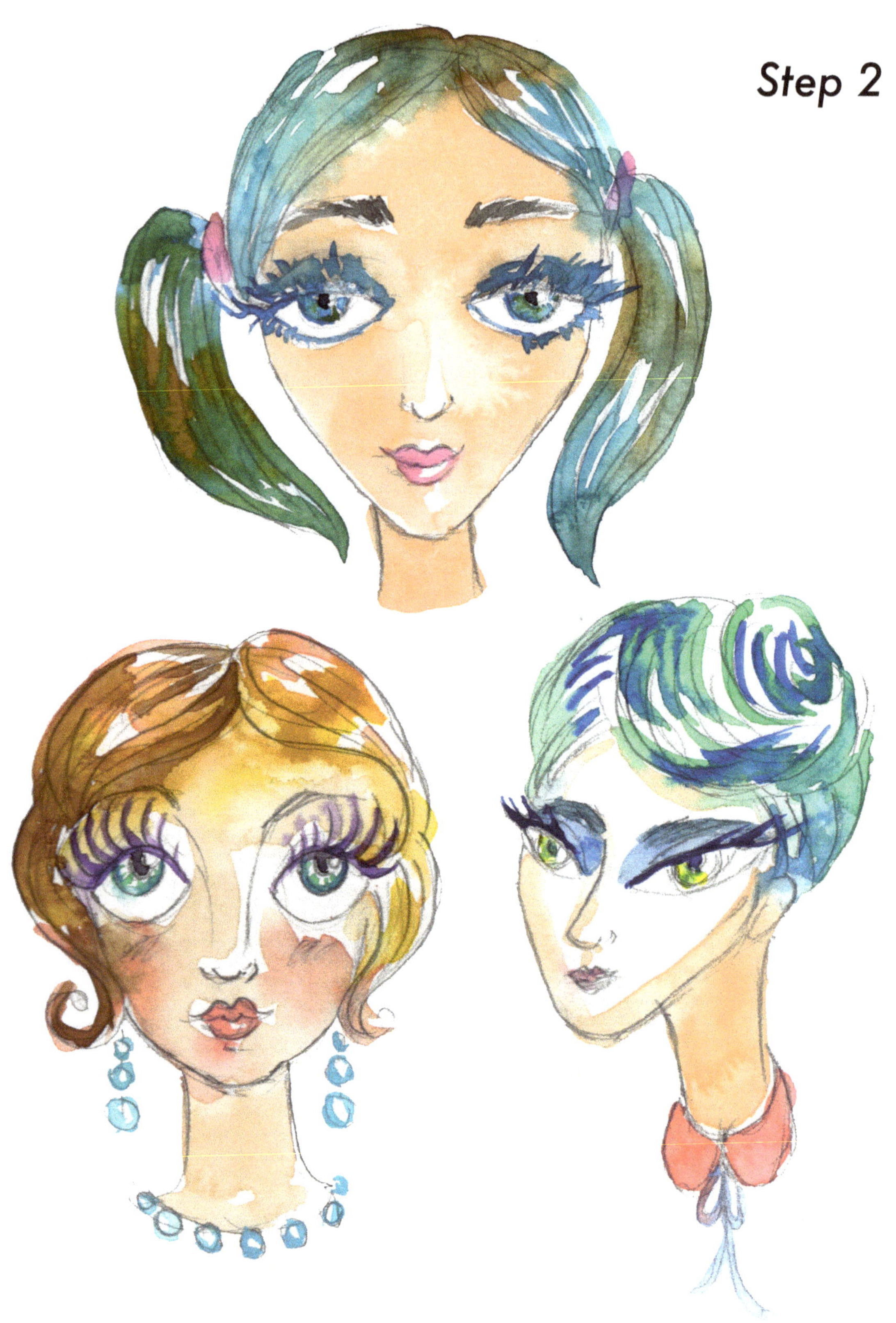

Let's apply the first watercolor layer. Here we are using bright jewel tones for the hair. Let colors run into each other in some areas, like hair and cheeks. Play with various colors for the eyes, to make them stand out.

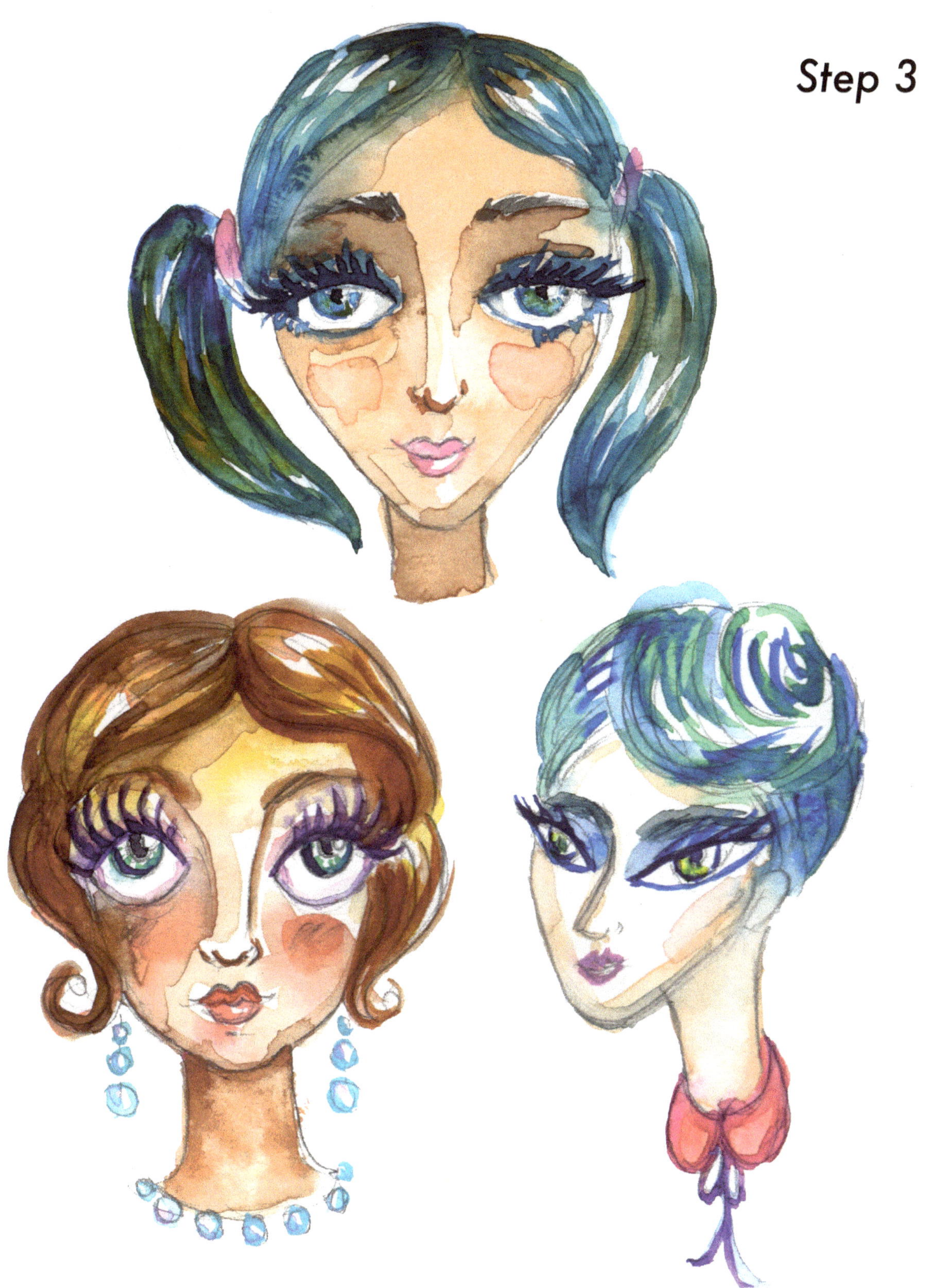

As a final step, let's apply another layer of watercolor, once the first layer has dried. Emphasize the eyelashes, to enhance the big eyes even further. Add shading by applying darker shades of the skin tone. Add blush.

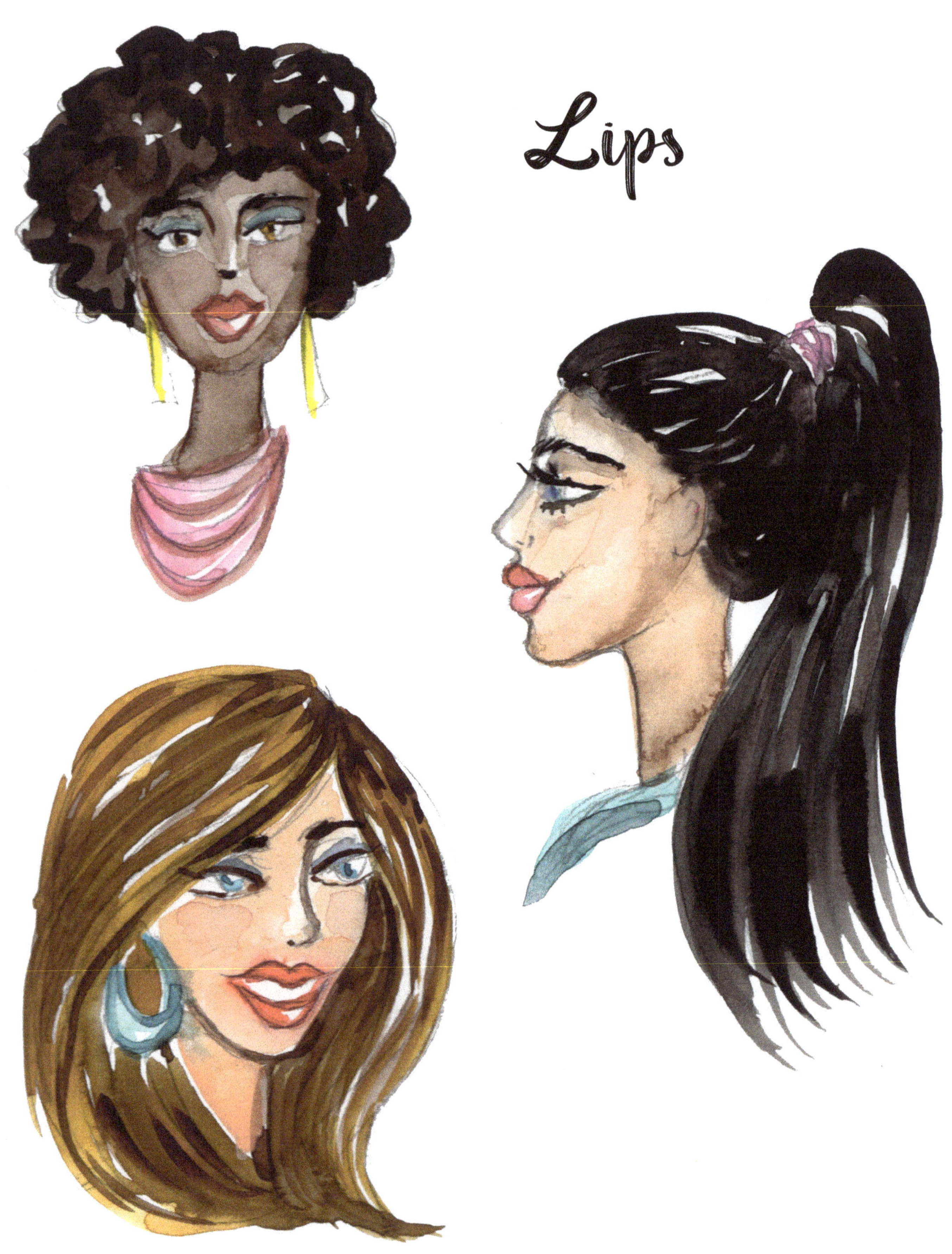

Lips

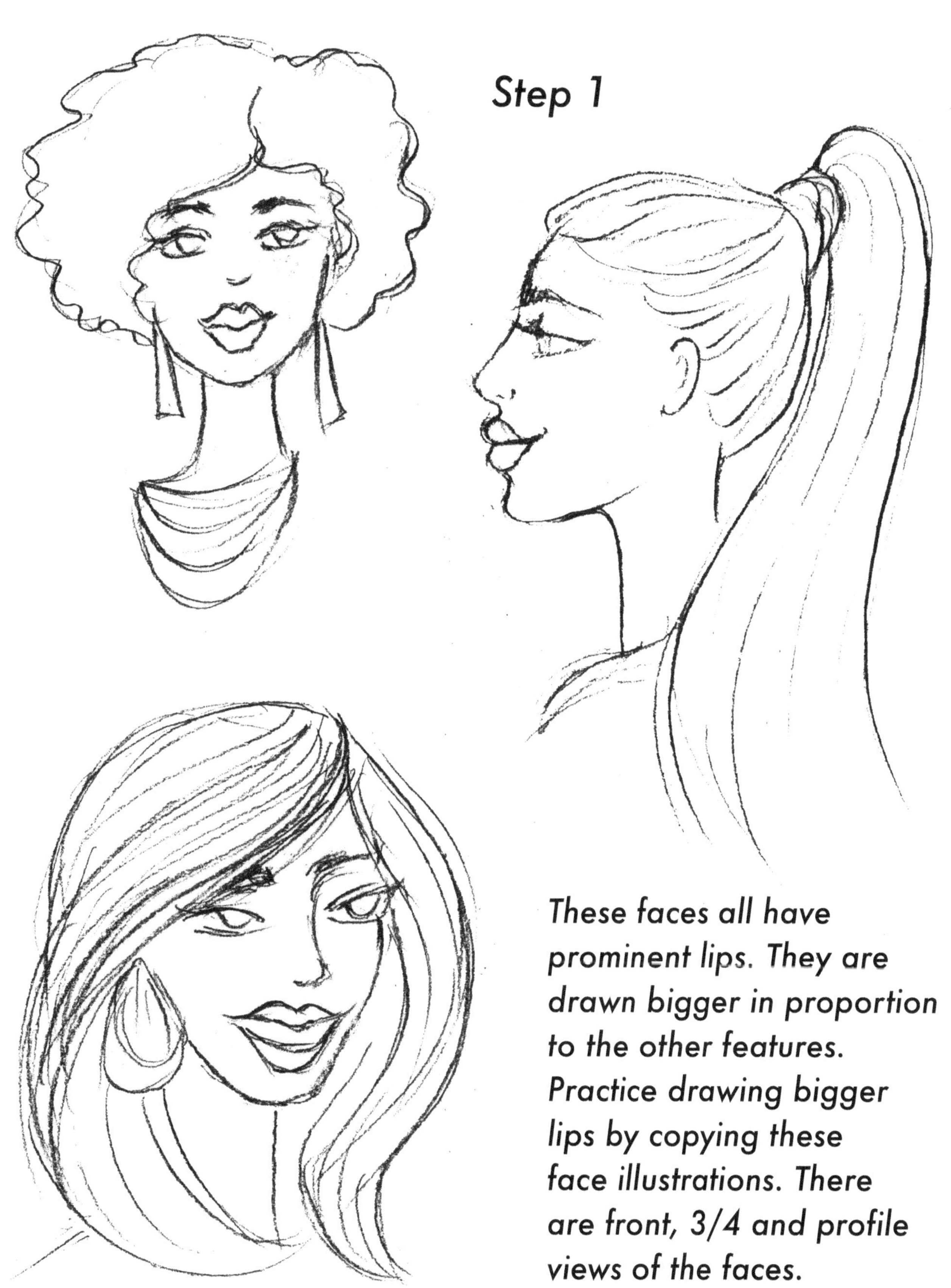

These faces all have prominent lips. They are drawn bigger in proportion to the other features. Practice drawing bigger lips by copying these face illustrations. There are front, 3/4 and profile views of the faces.

Step 2

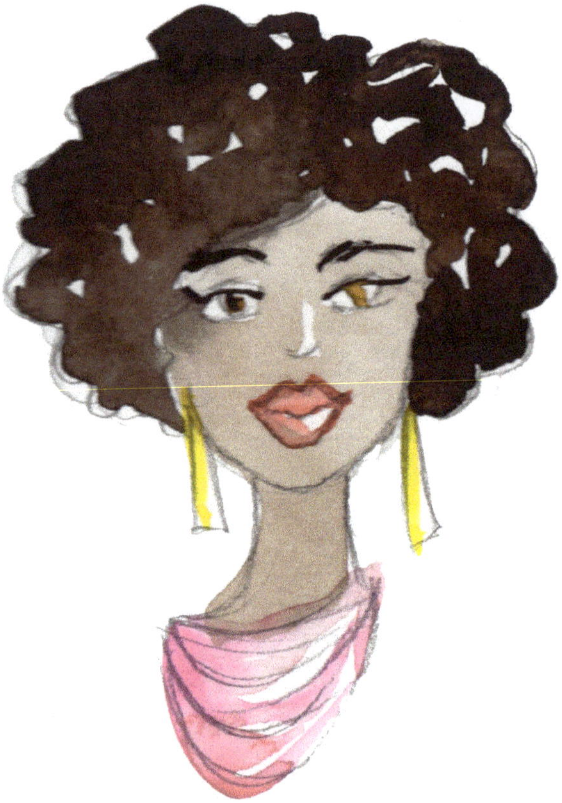

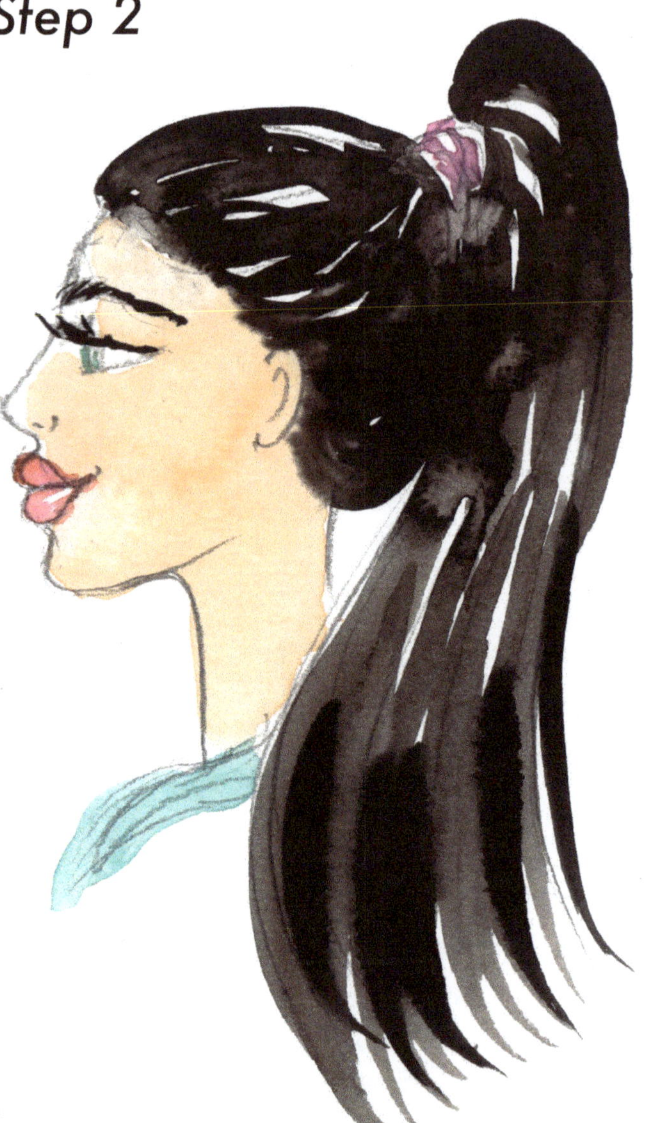

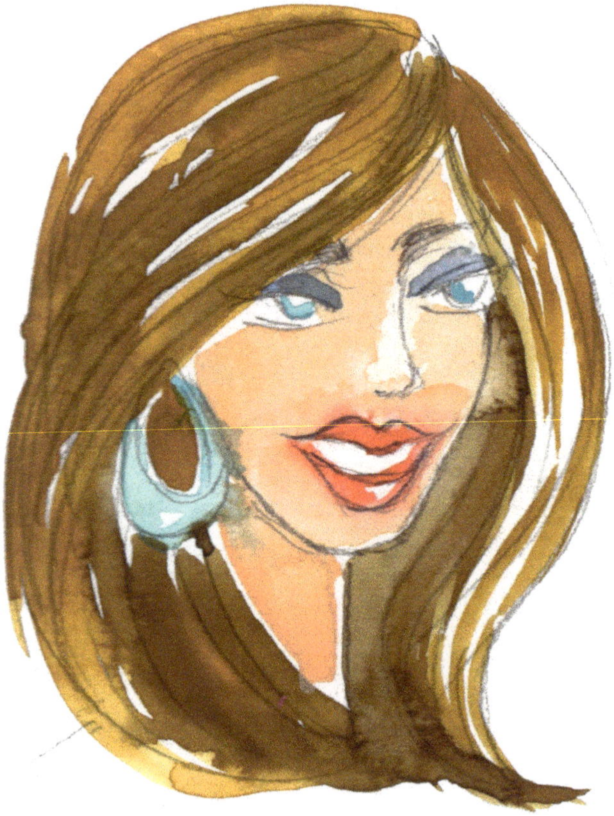

Let's apply the first
watercolor layer.
Note the highlights created
by leaving the white of the paper.
Dab off extra water or color
with a tissue or paper towel.
You can vary the skin tone
and hair colors. Feel free to test
the colors first before application.

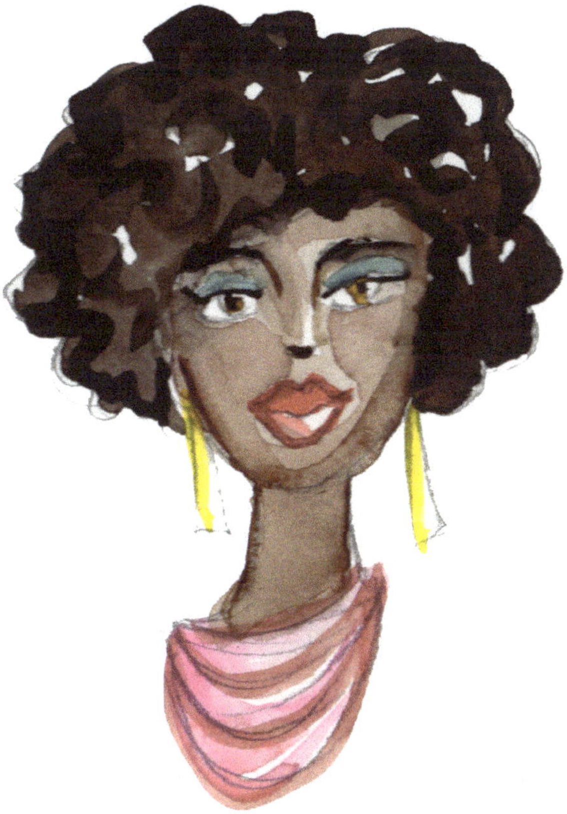

Step 3

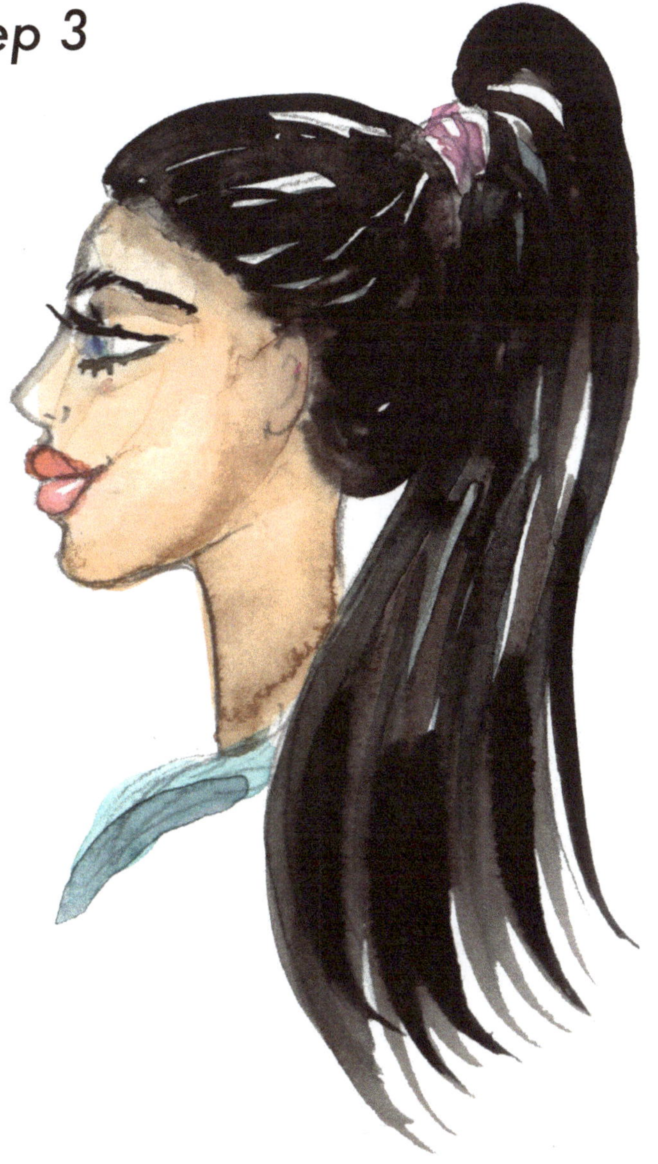

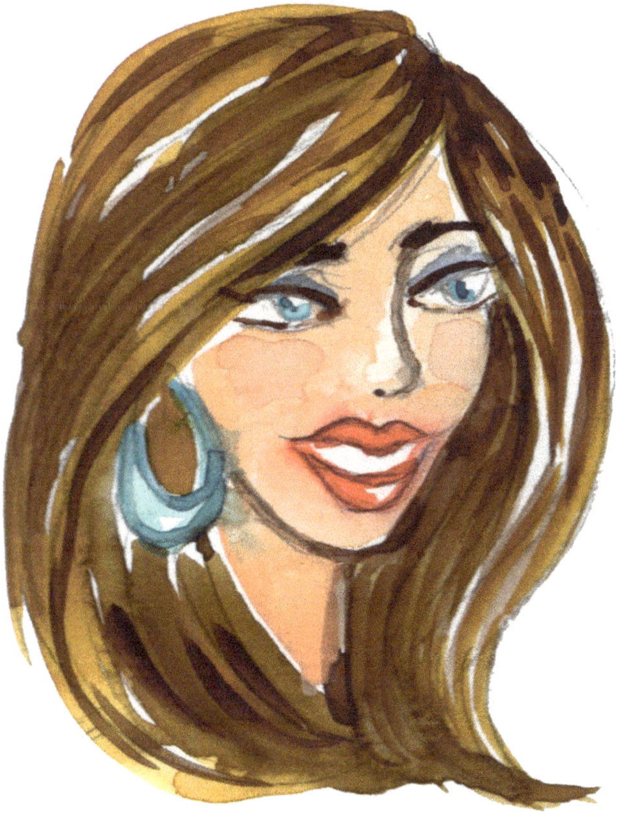

Once the first layer of watercolor dries, we can apply another layer. Here we can add more dimension and shading to our faces.
We can add texture to the hair, parts of clothing and jewelry.

Noses

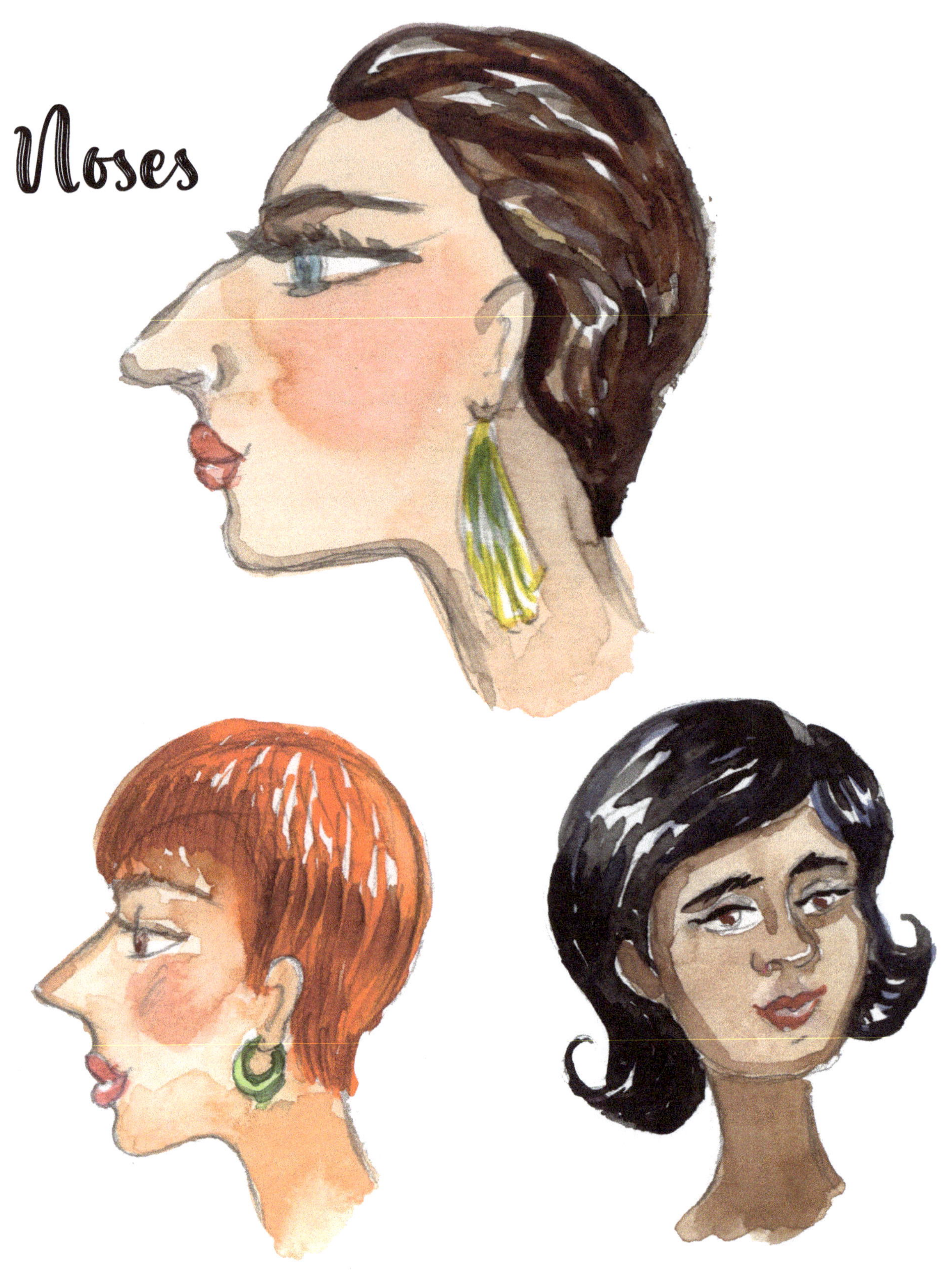

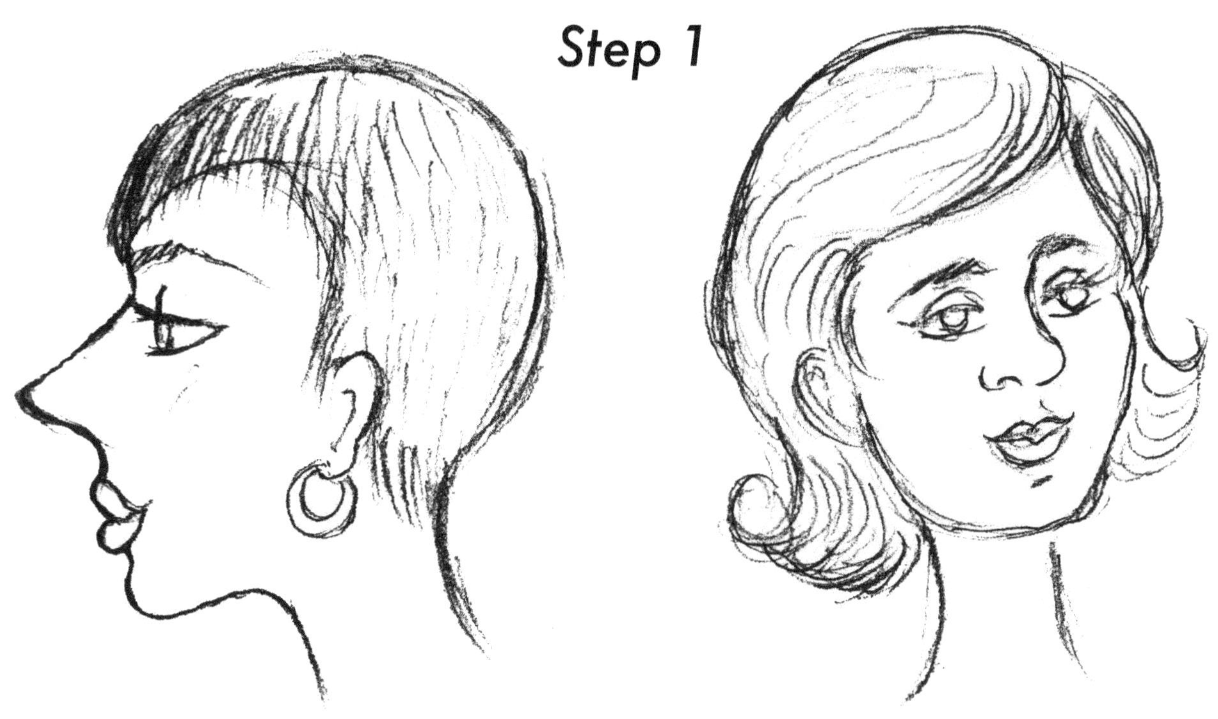

The following faces, all feature unique nose shapes of different types. There are two profile views and one 3/4 view.
Sketch these faces as you see them here. Feel free to exaggerate the noses.

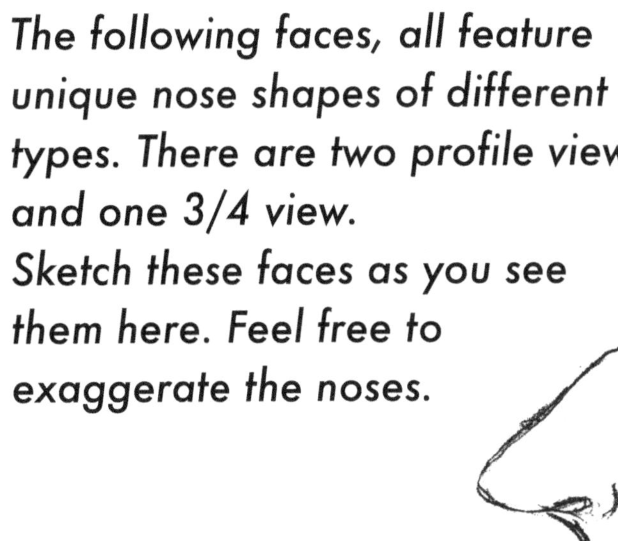

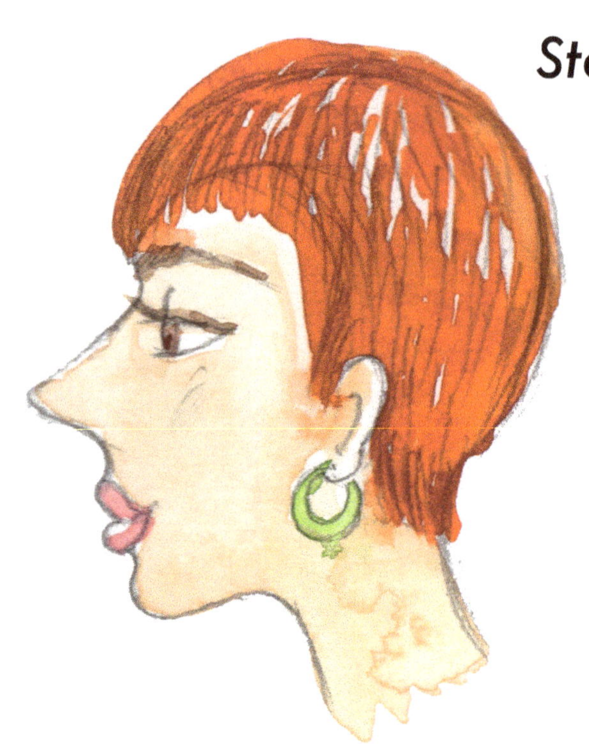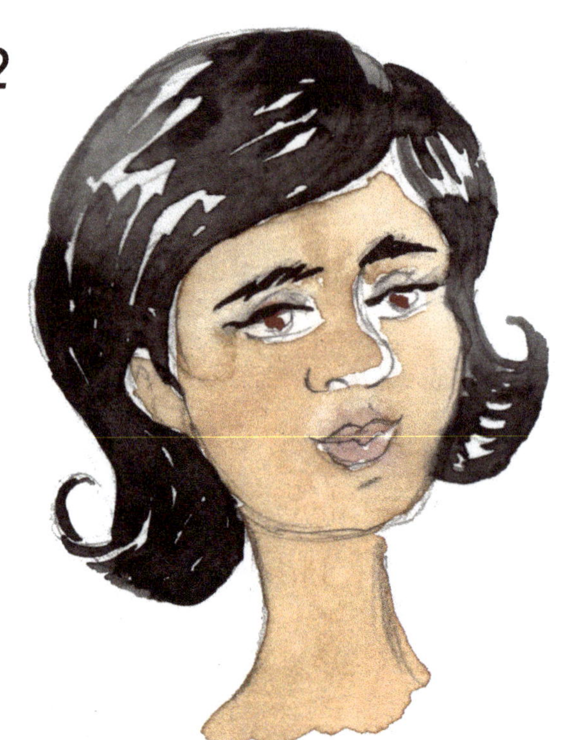

Now let us apply a layer of watercolor. Leave the white of the paper for highlights as you see in the examples. Jewelry, such as earrings can enhance our portraits and emphasize the unique look of each face.

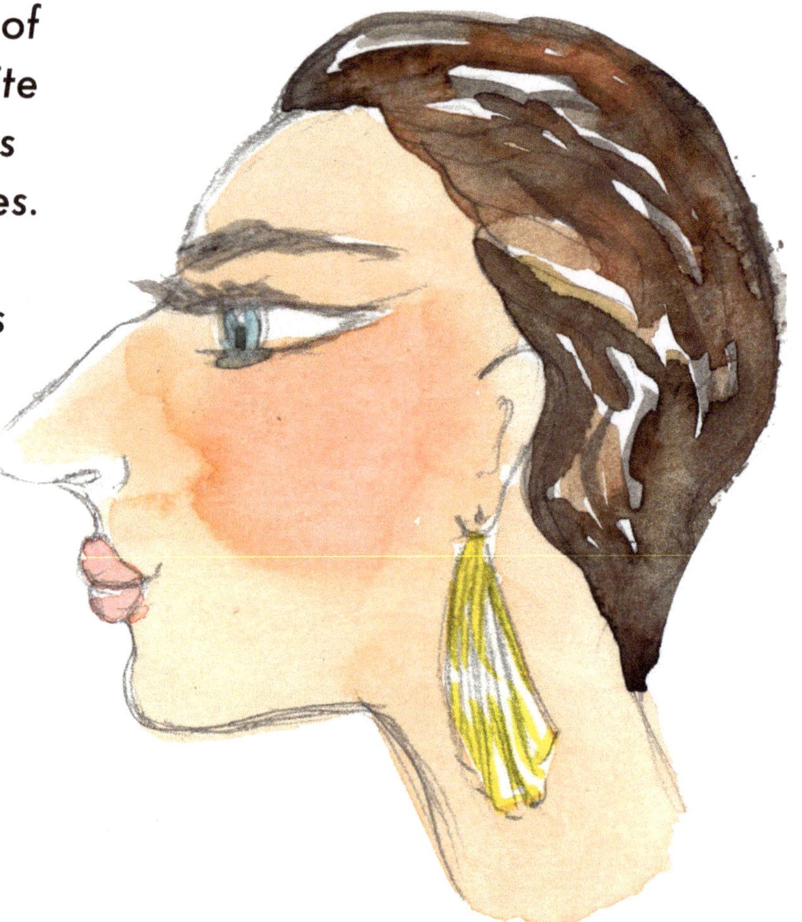

Step 3

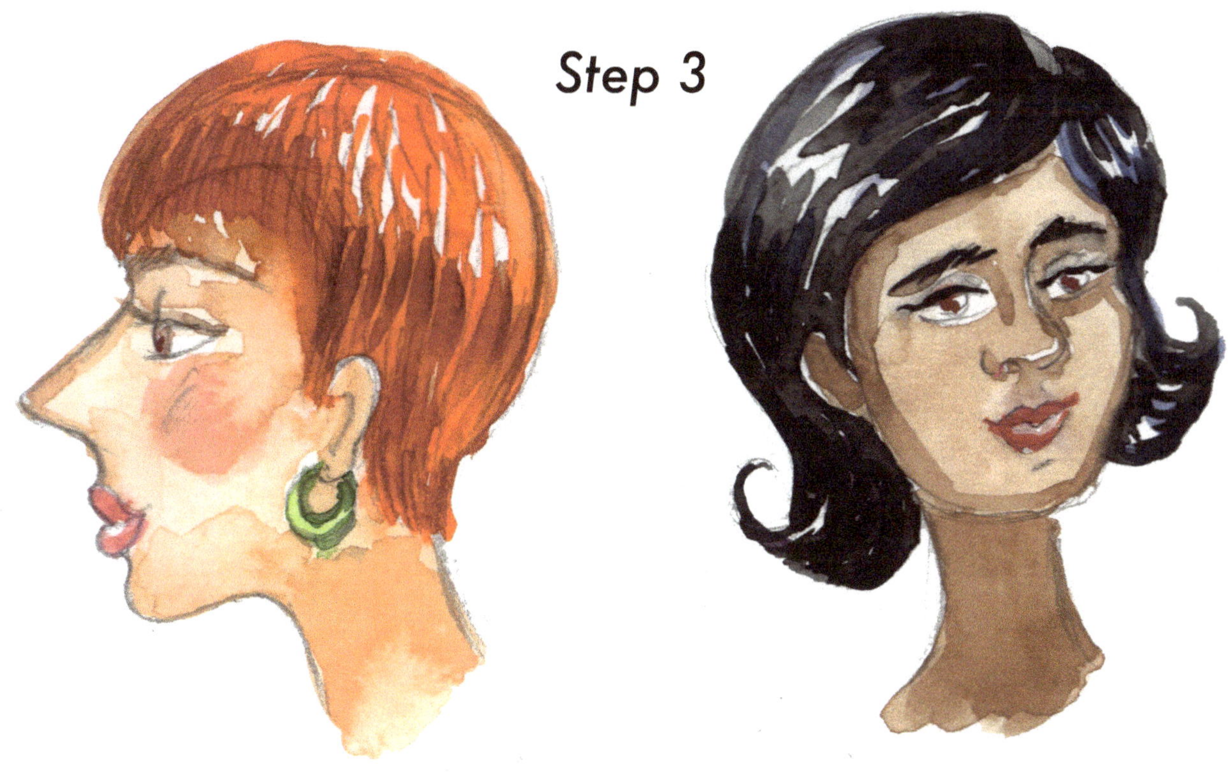

For the final watercolor layer, we can go into further details in the faces and the hair. Note the way the hair has more depth and variation of colors. Use darker shades of the skin tones to add as an outline around the faces.

Flower Girl Portrait

Now, let us go over the steps of painting creative, fun, unique and vibrant faces. For this exercise, let's dive right into painting a straight watercolor portrait, skipping pre-drawing with a pencil. Begin by mixing the flesh tone of your choice with water. Using a large brush, paint the oval of the face and the neck.

Step 1

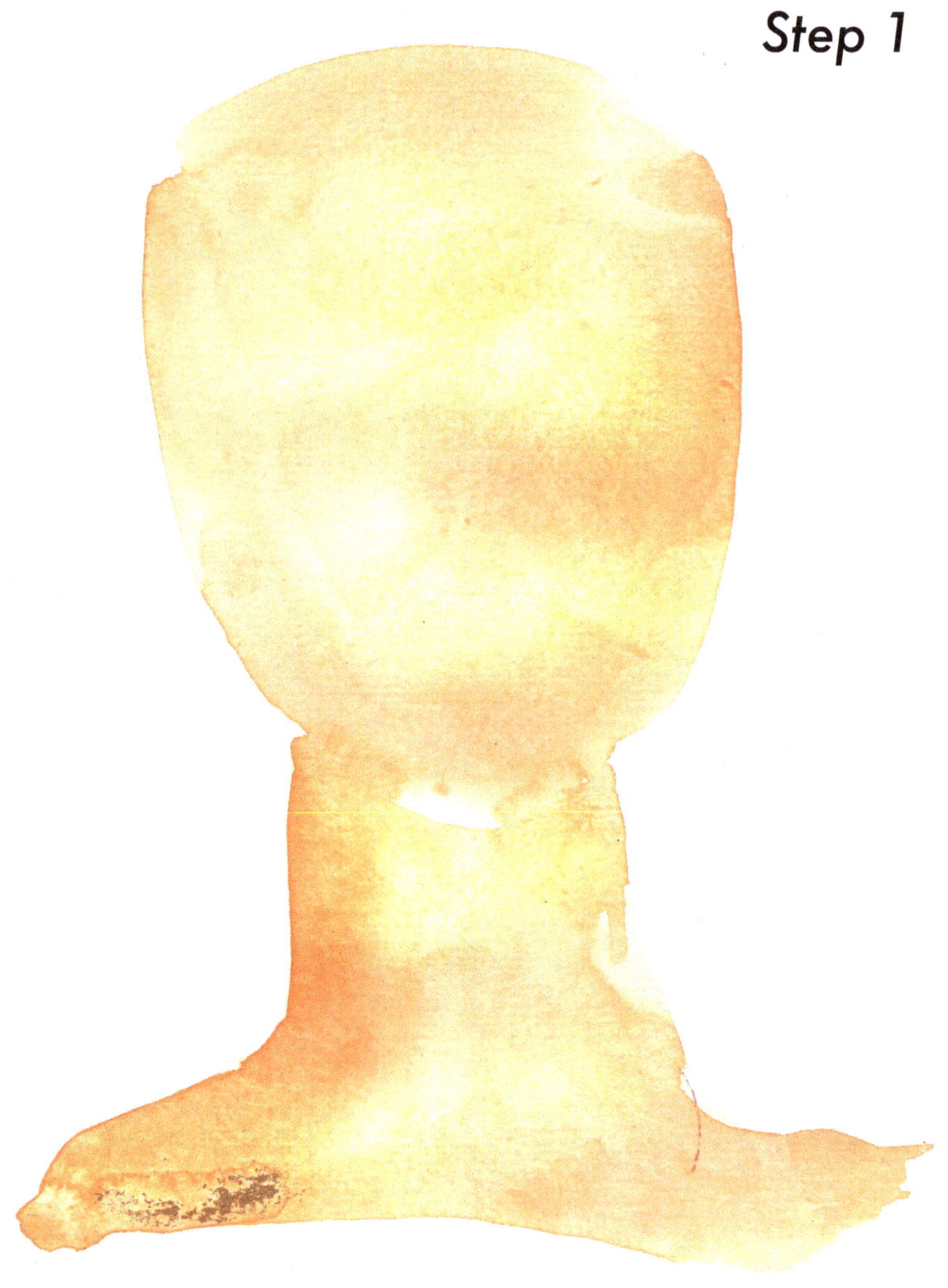

Now, using a thinner brush, create loose flower drawings with a variety of colors of your choosing. Copy the shapes of the flowers and leaves or make up your own.

Step 2

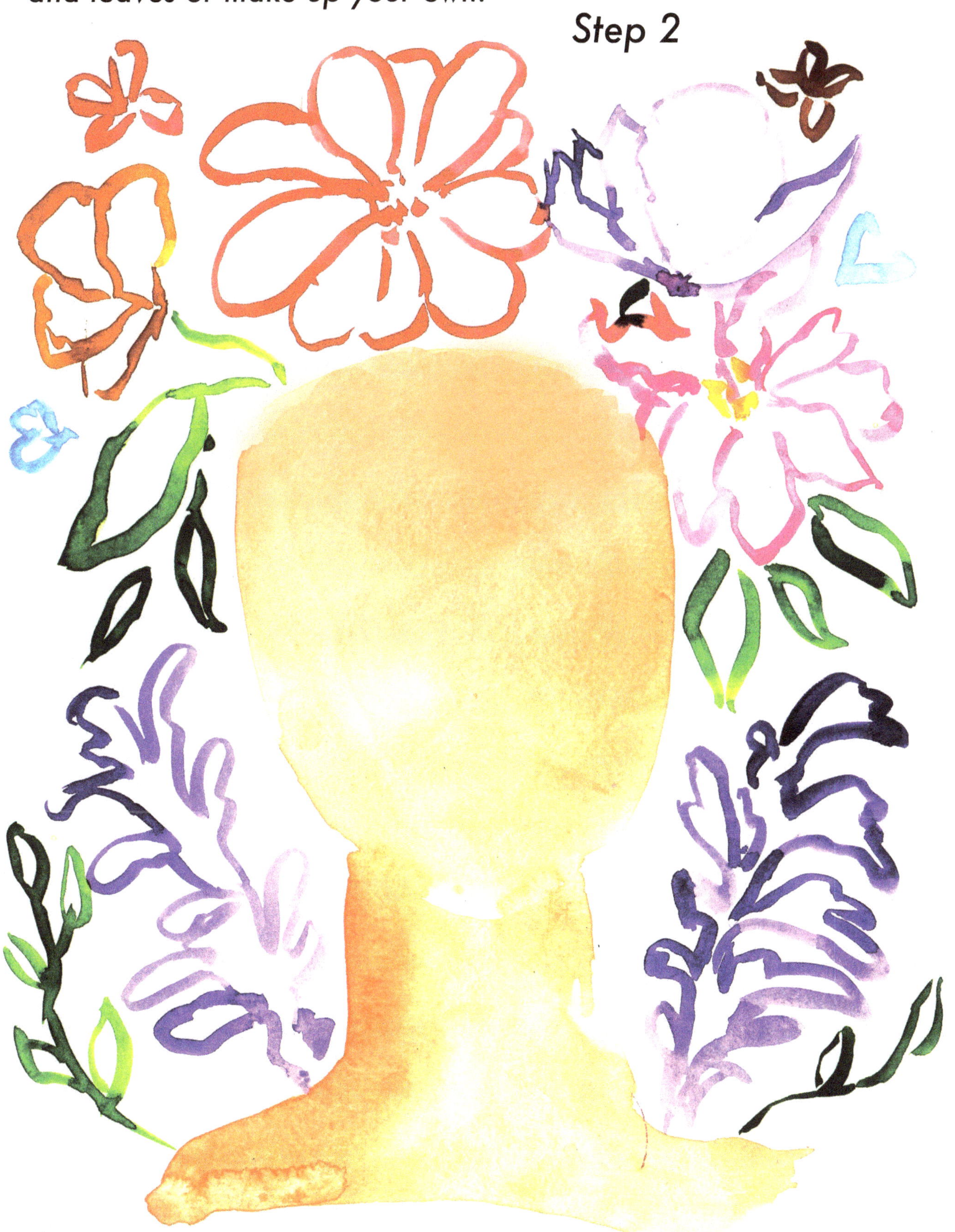

Once this layer has dried, let's give her facial features, as you see below. Then color in the flowers. Let the colors bleed a bit for the nice loose watercolor look.

Step 3

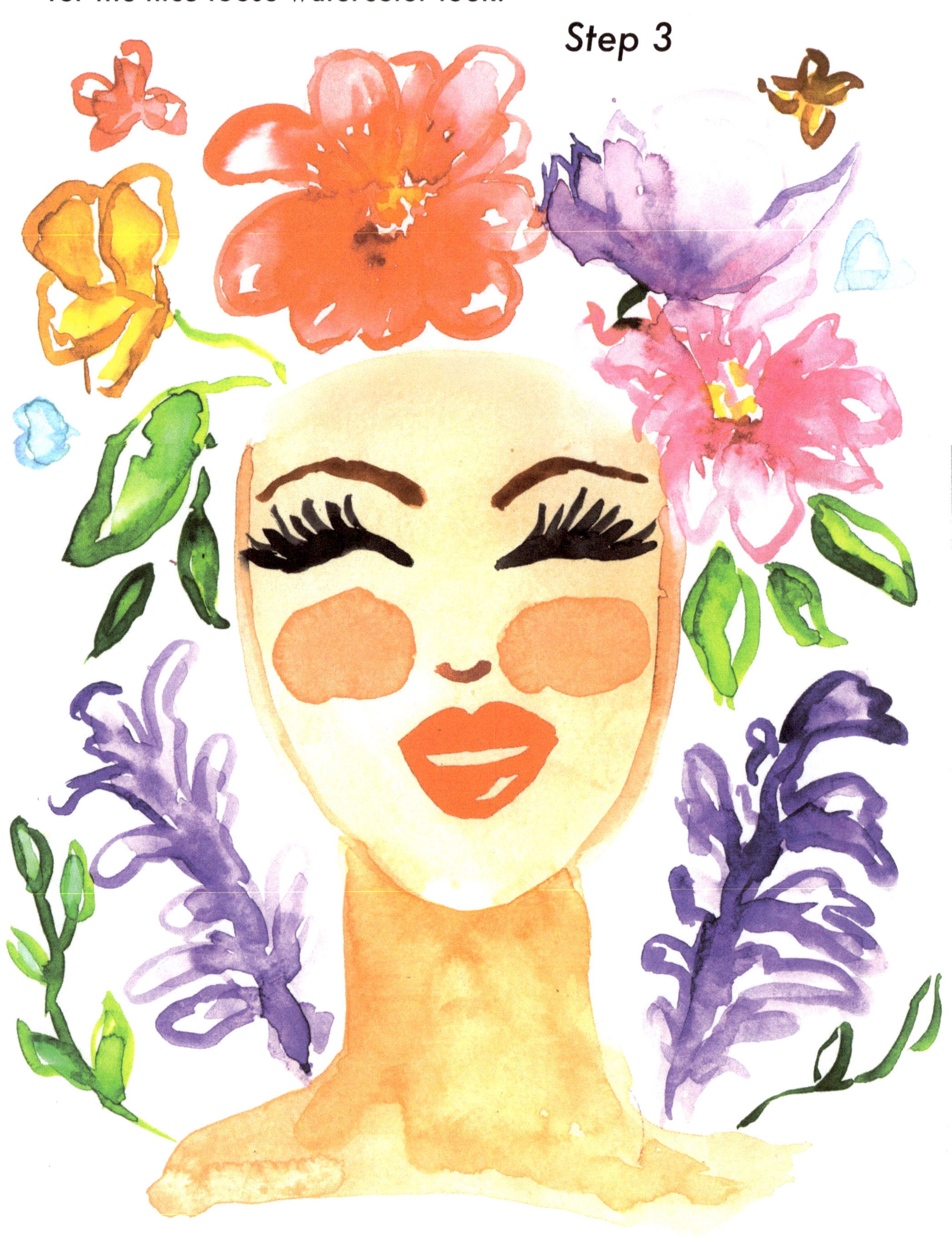

Step 4

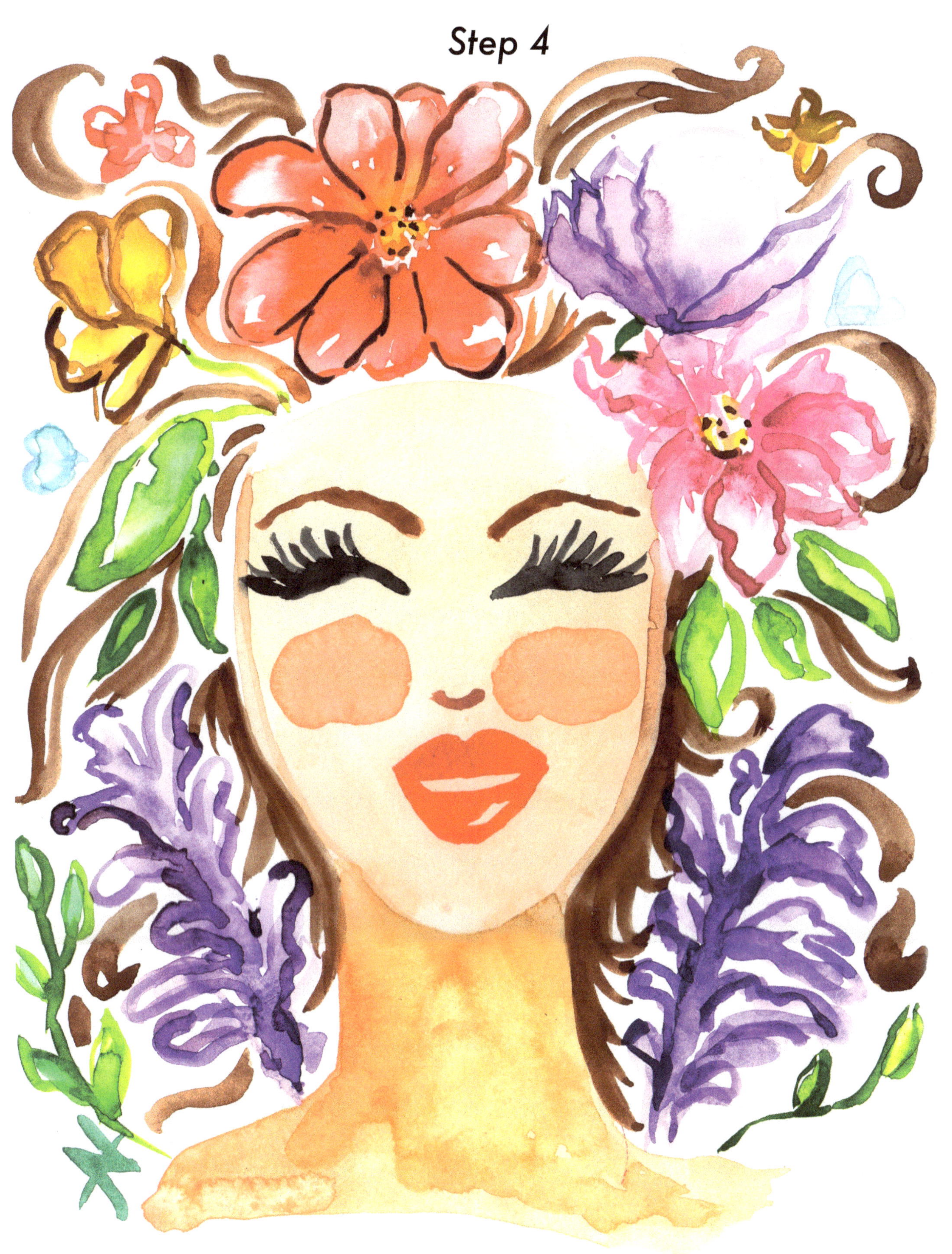

Once this layer has dried, add final touches, lines and shadows.

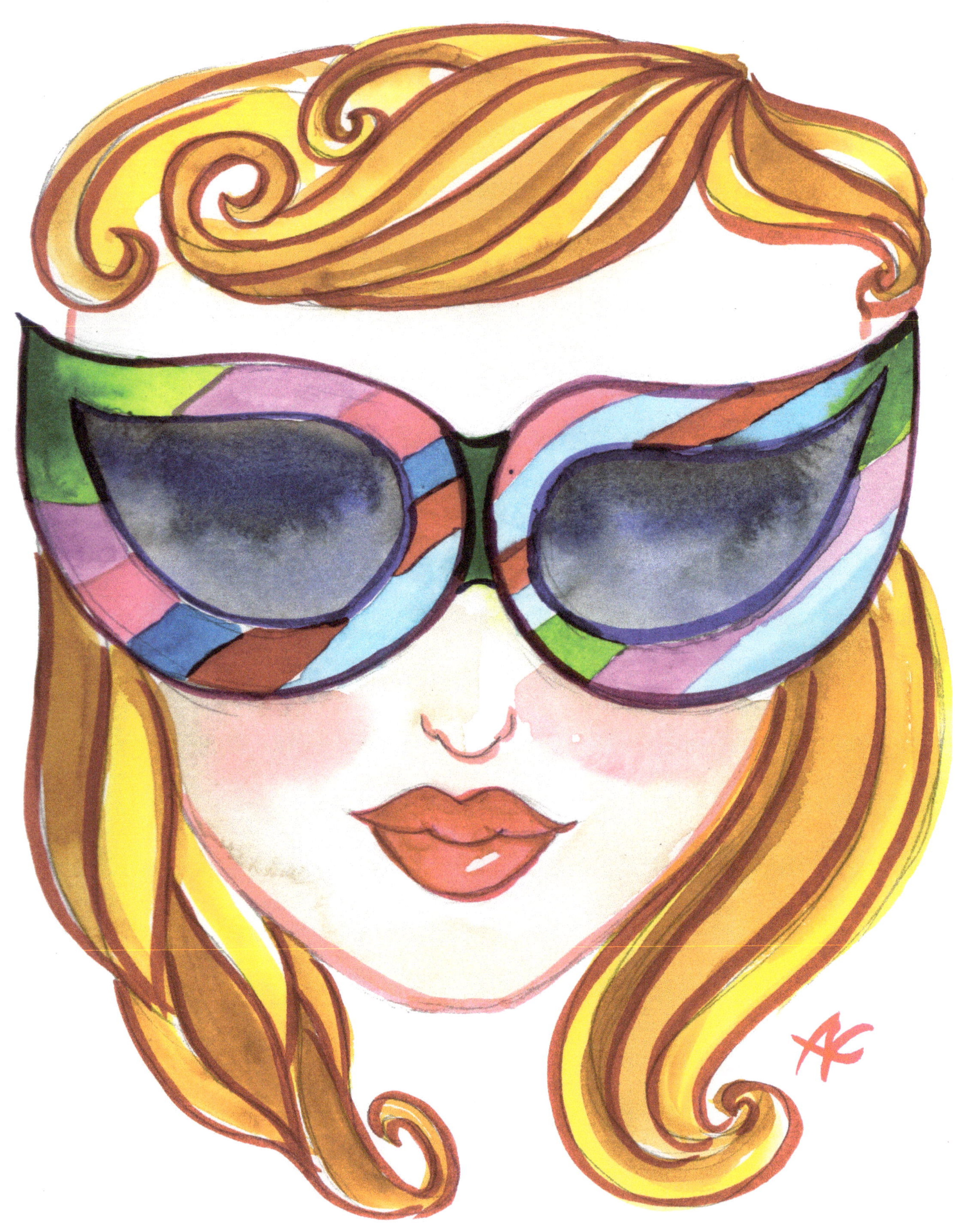

Cat Eye Sunglasses Girl

Let's make a fun illustration of a girl in cat eye sunglasses. Sketch the face below. Use smooth, flowing lines when you draw hair.

Step 1

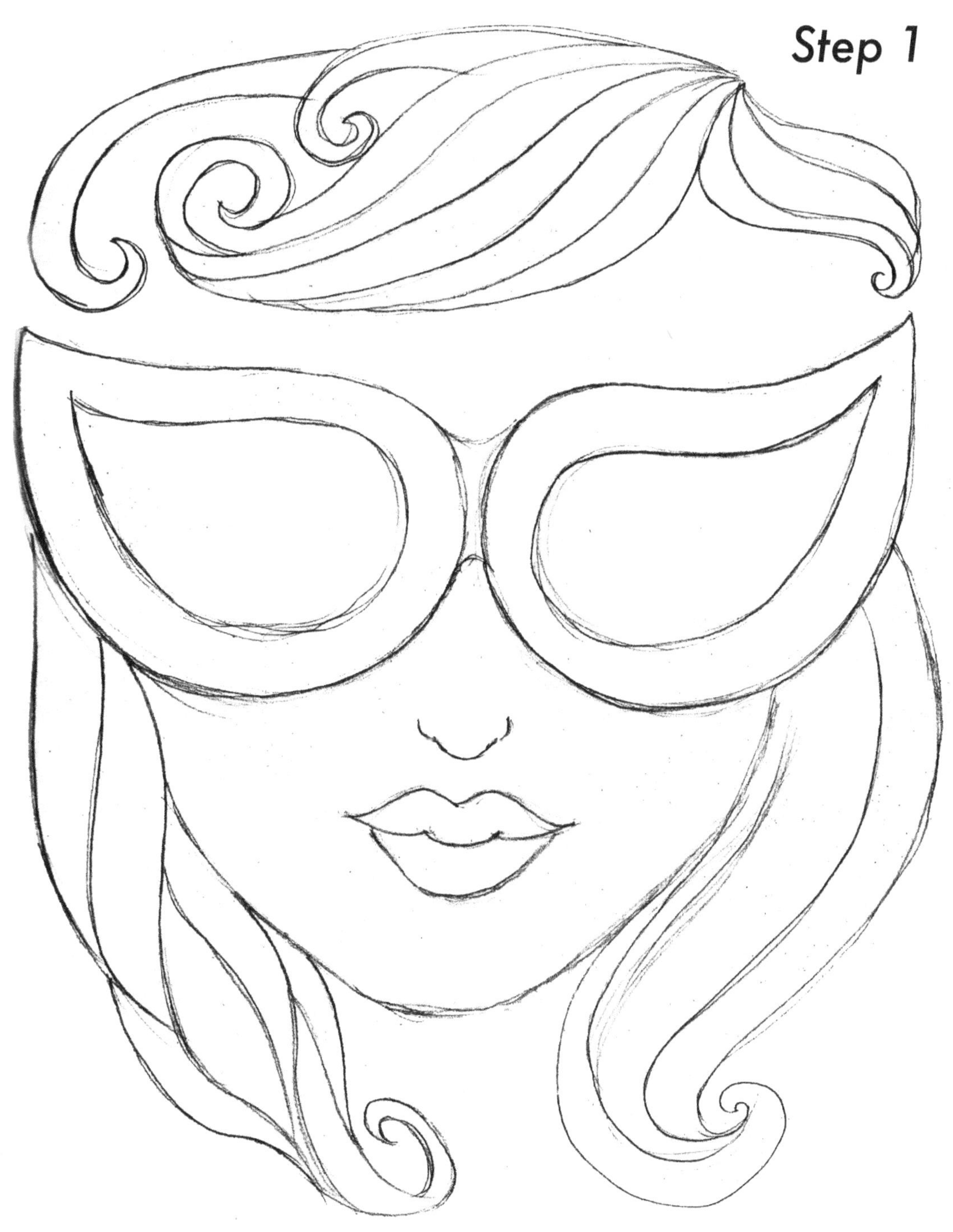

Now let's paint! Apply the watercolors in generous strokes, following the lines of the hair. Use varying shades - yellow and yellow ocre for darker spots. Use colors of your choice for the glasses. Have fun with it! To make the lenses, use gradients of darker blue-gray to lighter blue-gray.

Step 2

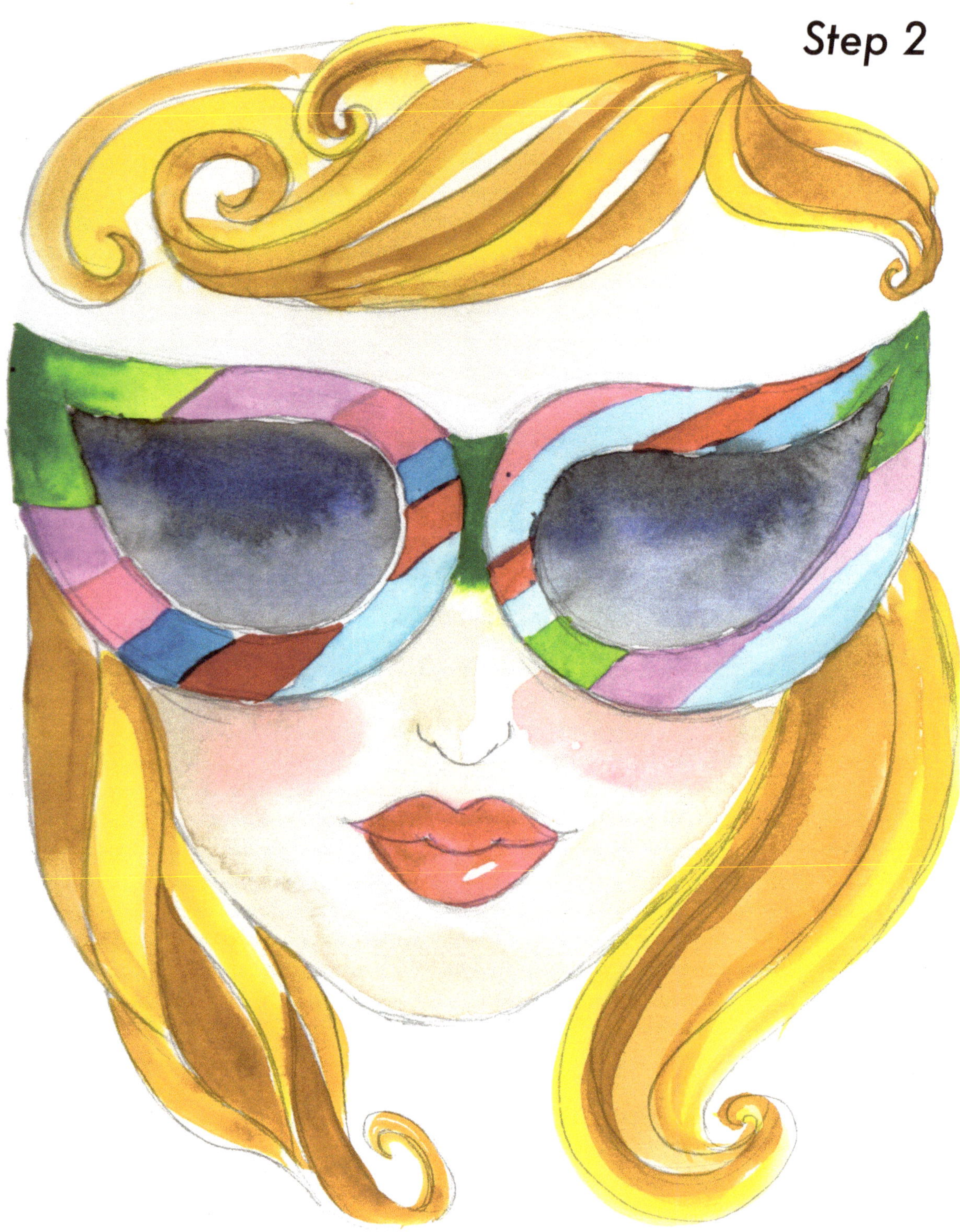

For this illustration, once our watercolor dries, we can outline the hair, glasses and face with brush markers. Use darker shades but those that are similar to the surrounding colors.

Step 3

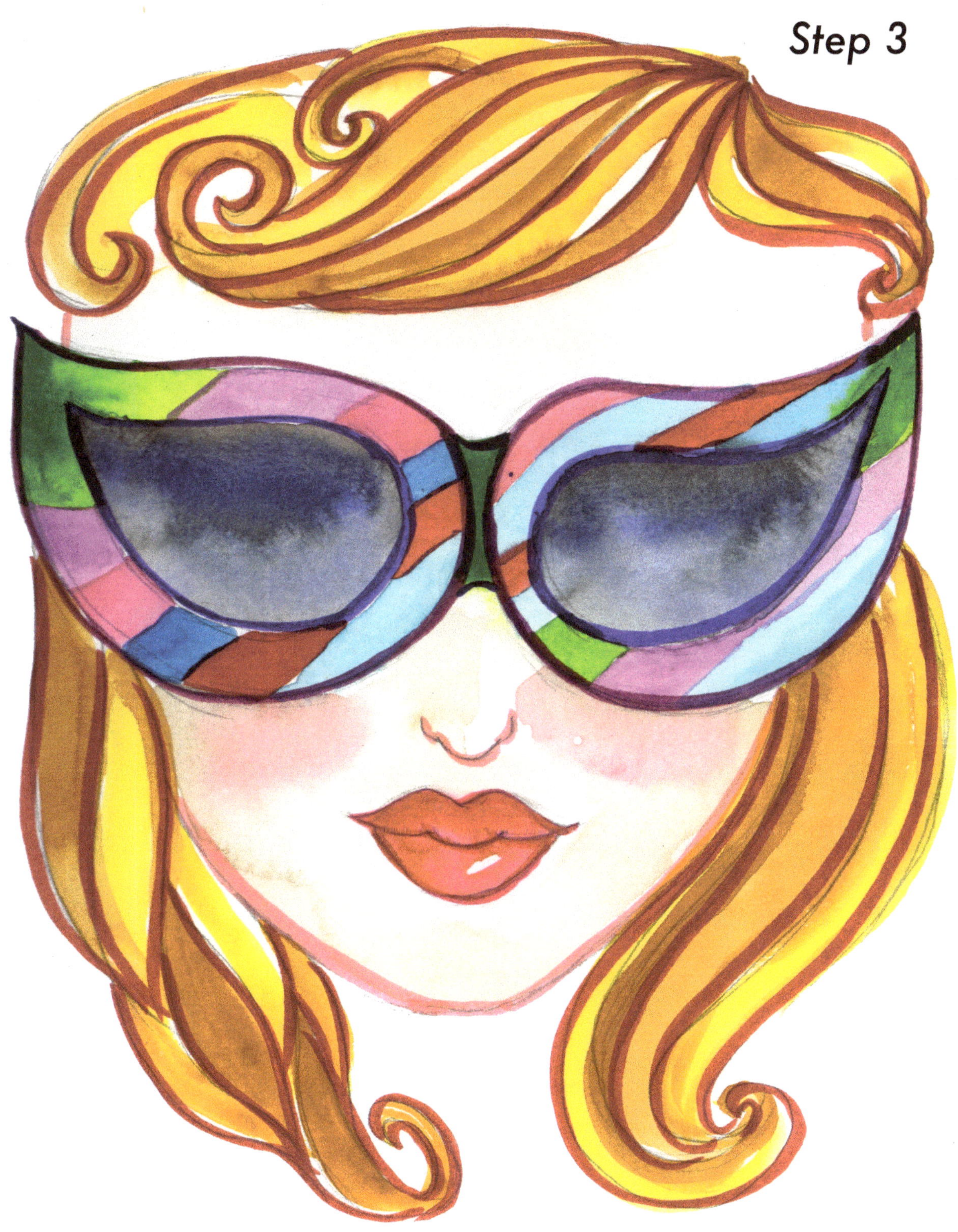

Geometric Girl

Let's make a fun illustration of a girl with angular features and accessories. This illustration is cropped on the sides, so let's put a frame around it.

Step 1

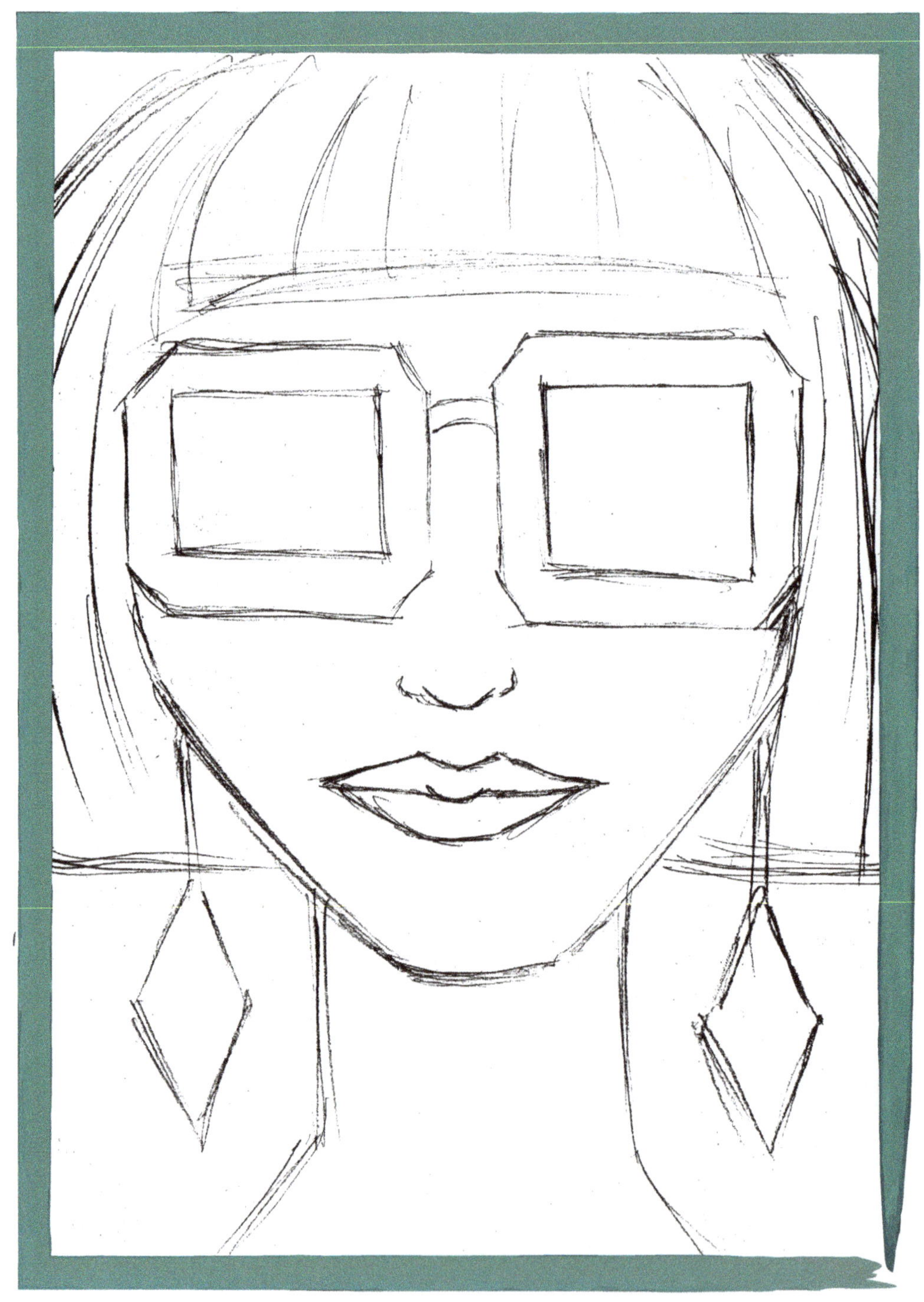

Now let's apply watercolor. Note how I showed highlights by leaving the white of the paper on the hair, as well as the lower lip. Use rich, vibrant colors for glasses and earrings.

Step 2

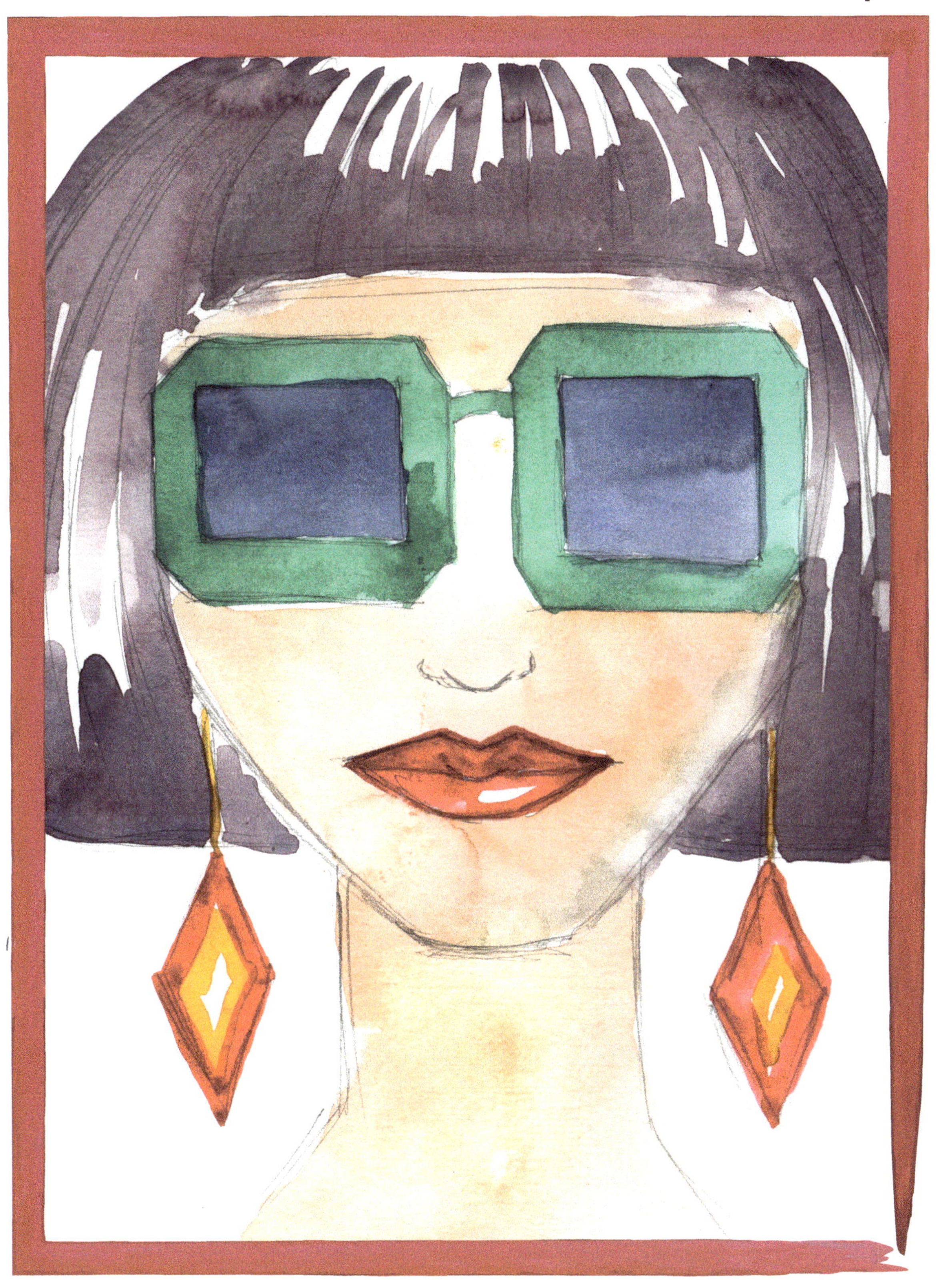

Once that layer has dried, apply another layer in spots.
Using a point of a brush, draw darker lines in the hair
with your watercolor, outline the face, shade the nose,
add a layer of color on the neck, and outline the glasses.

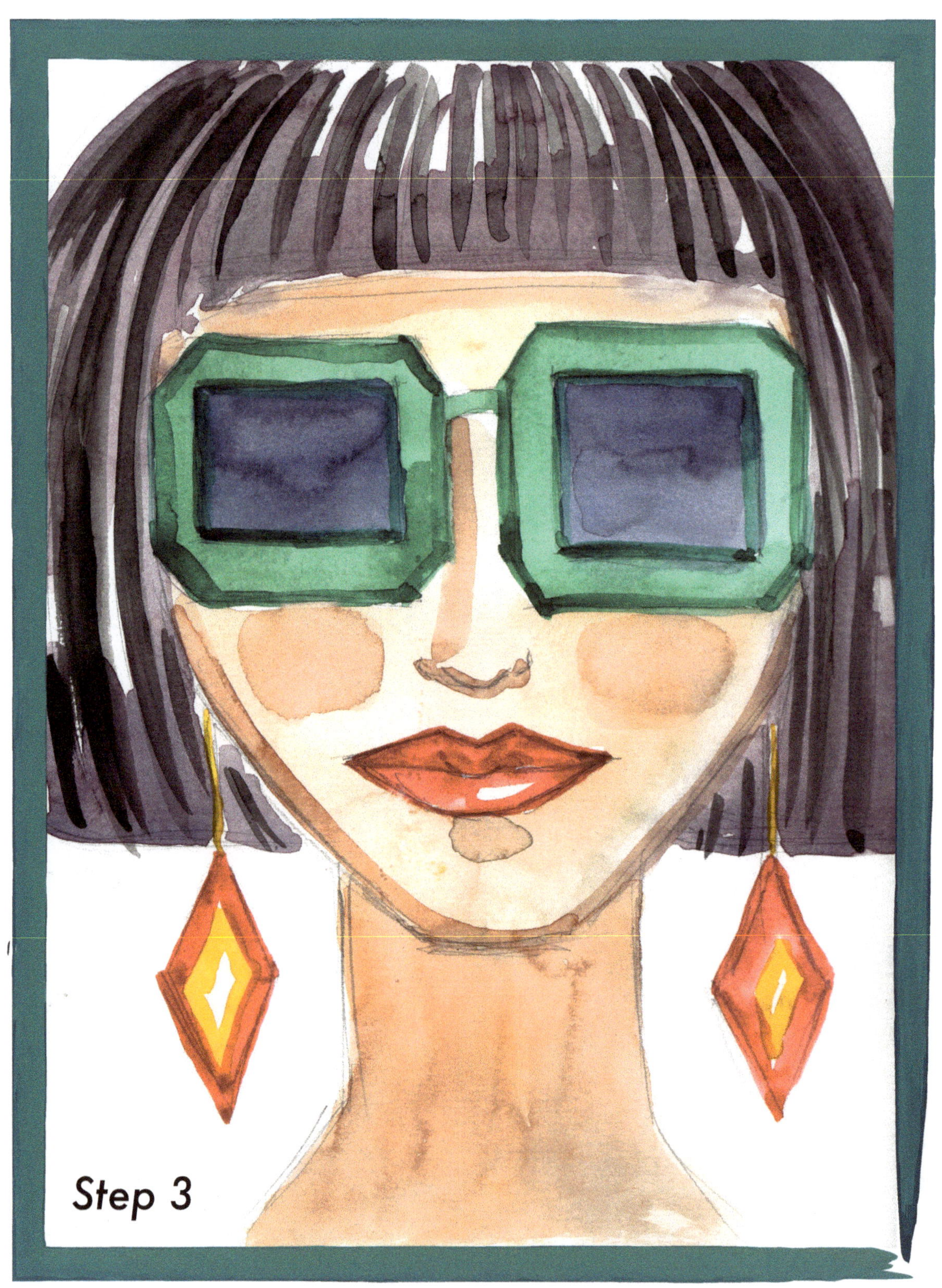

For this illustration, I decided to add accents with brush markers. Have fun with this step, by adding bold lines!

Step 4

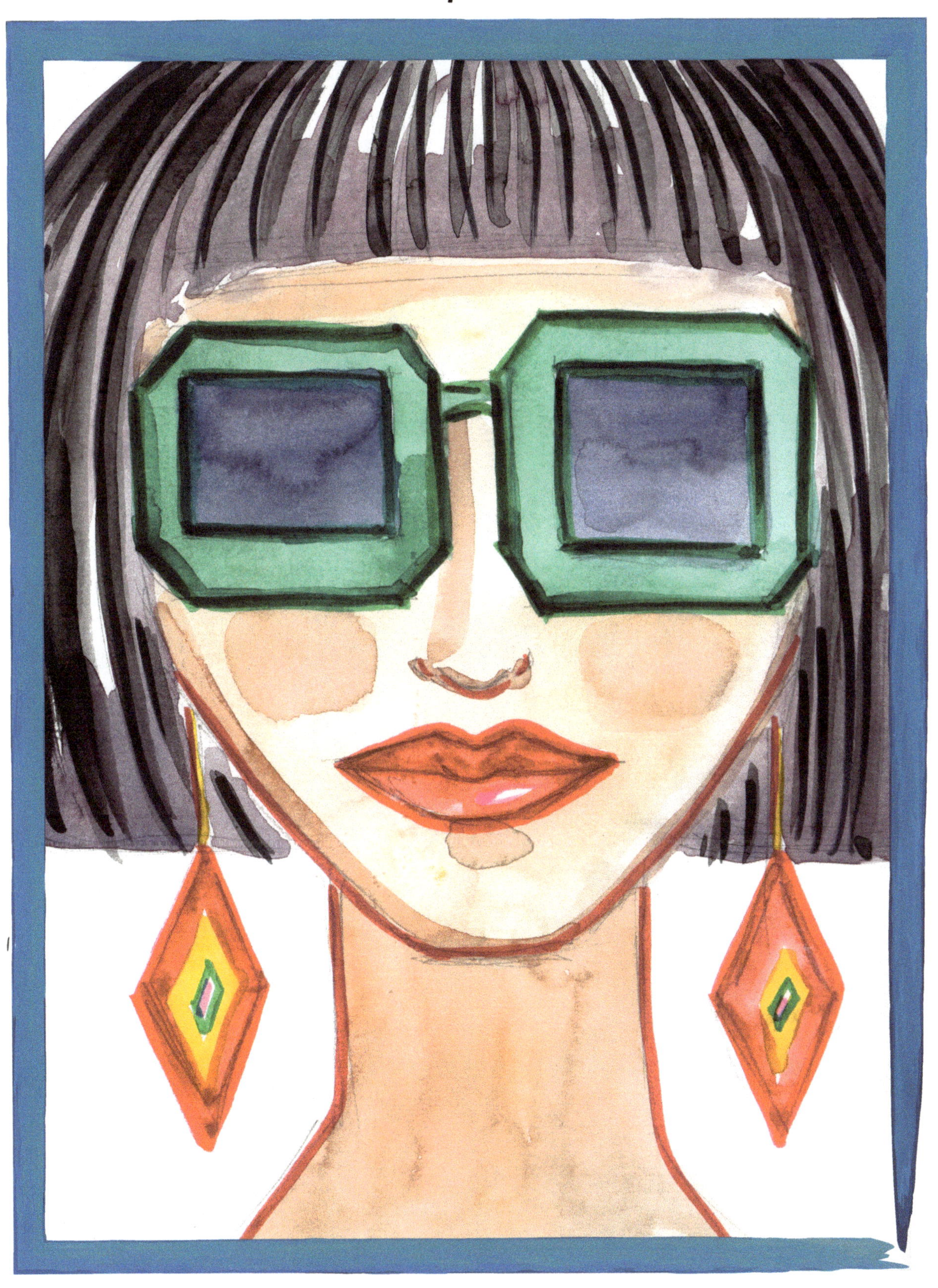

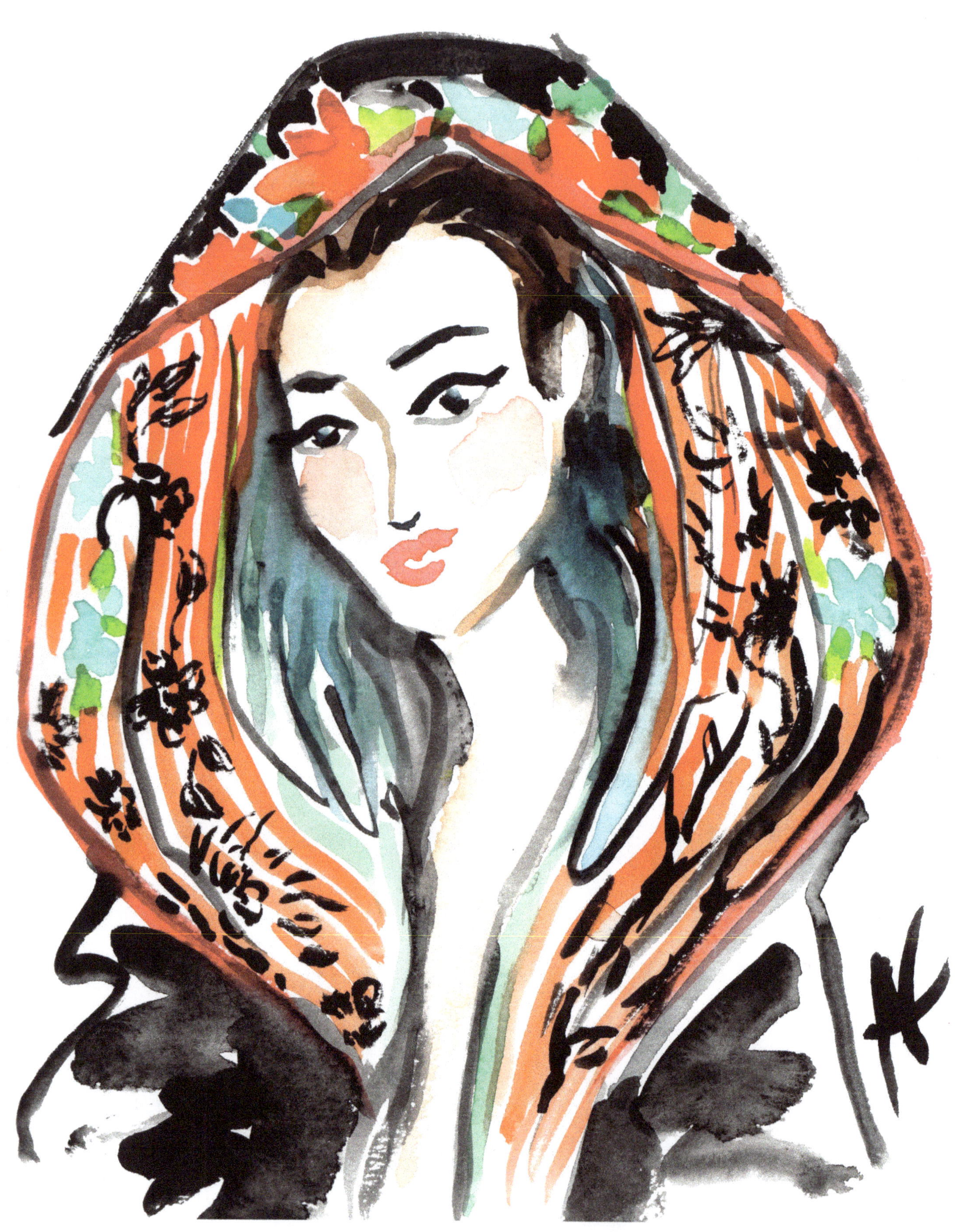

Drawing with Watercolor

For this exercise, we will draw and paint a portrait with straight watercolor, from a photograph.

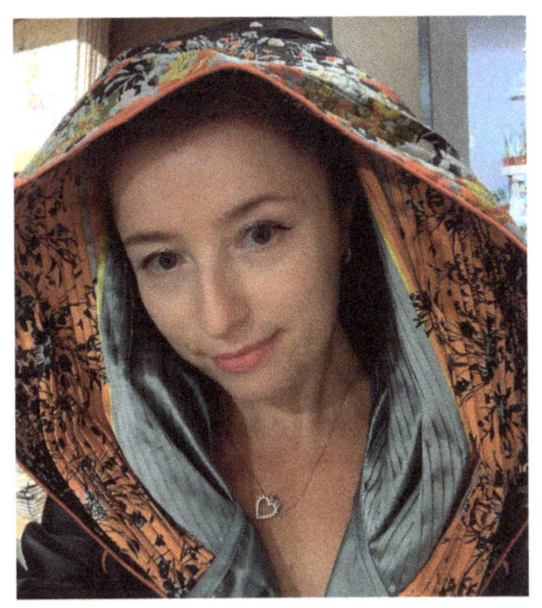

Step 1

Using a thin brush, draw the illustration from a reference photo. Loosely lay out the figure's shape. Here we have a person wearing a kimono-like coat. Add in parts that are cropped off in the photo. Simplify the facial features.

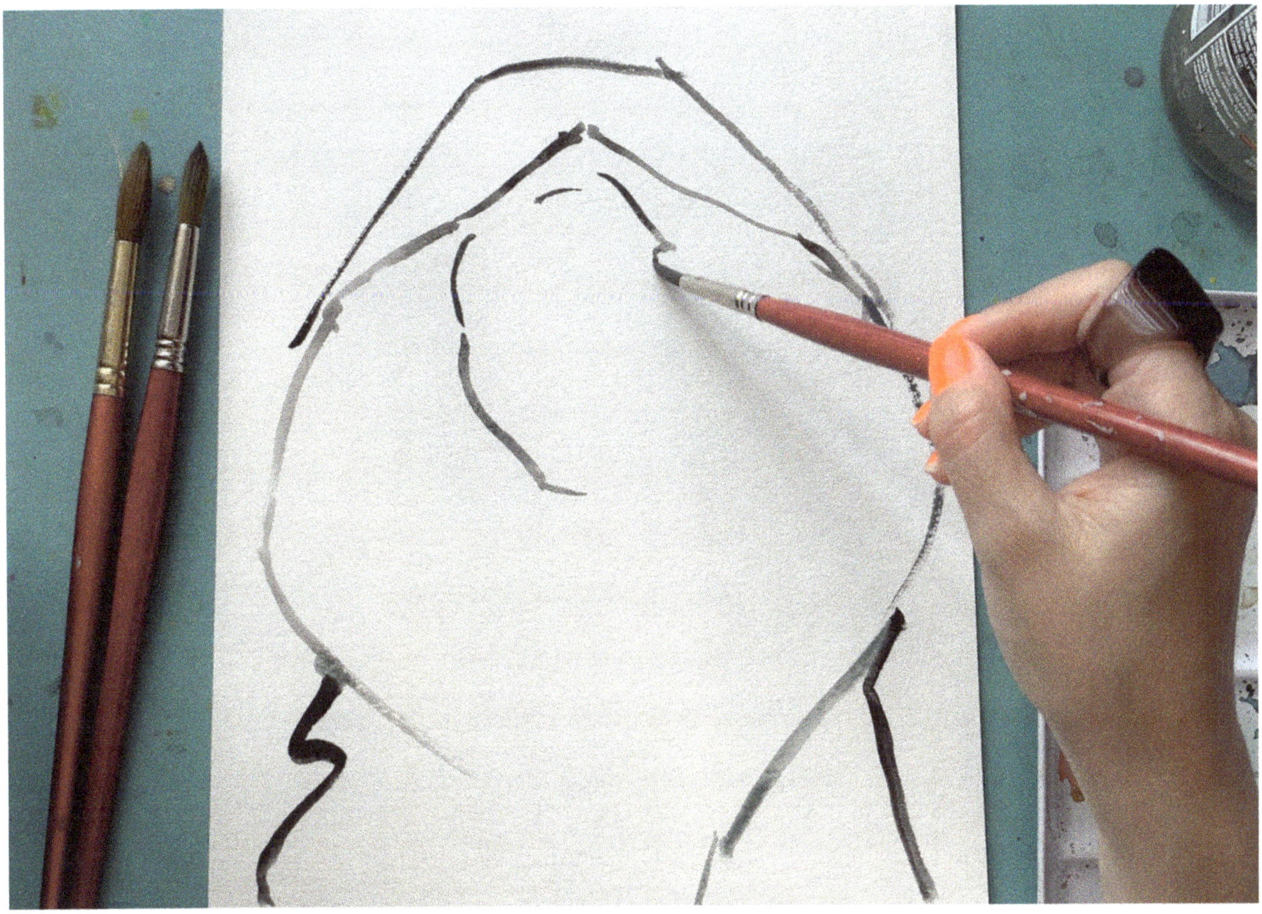

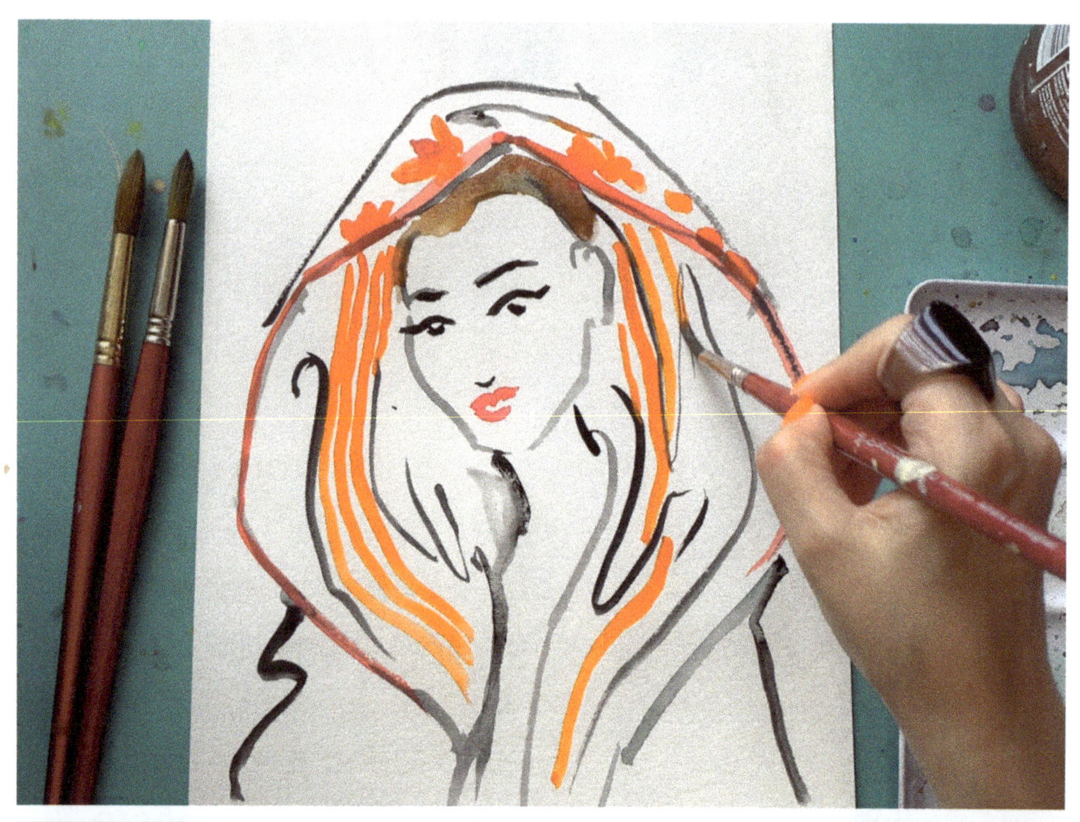

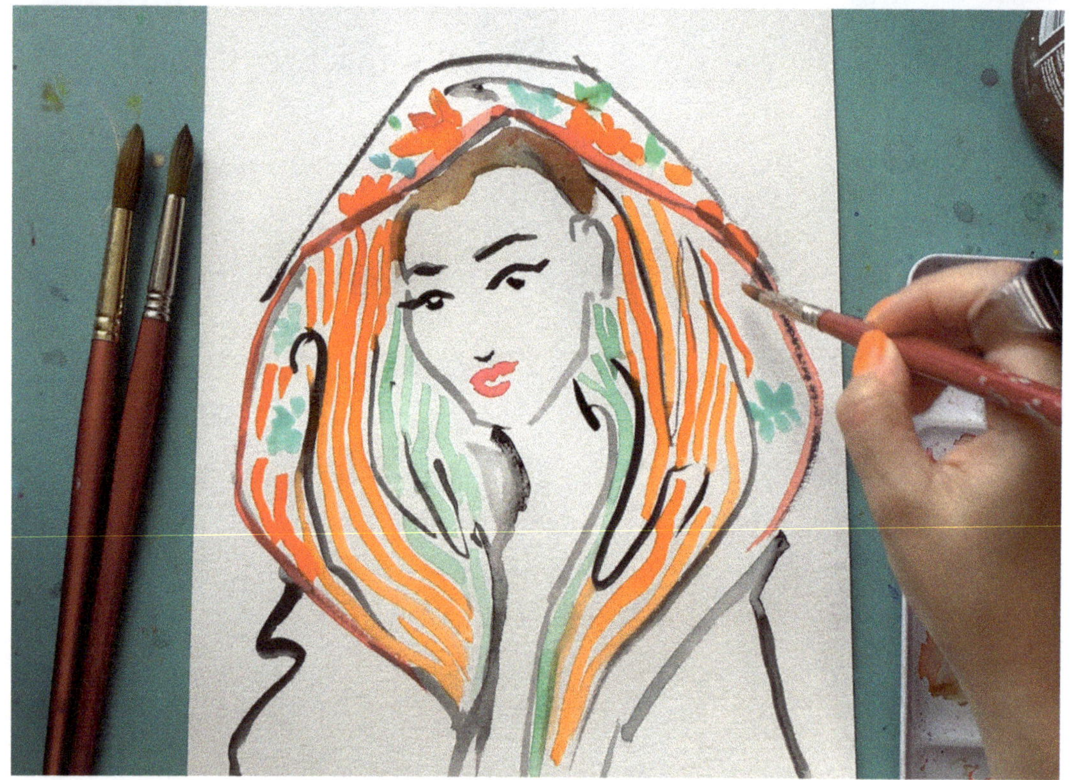

Add in the patterns. Feel free to take liberties in your interpretation of the pattern. Note how it changes with the folds. Use vibrant colors that stand out.

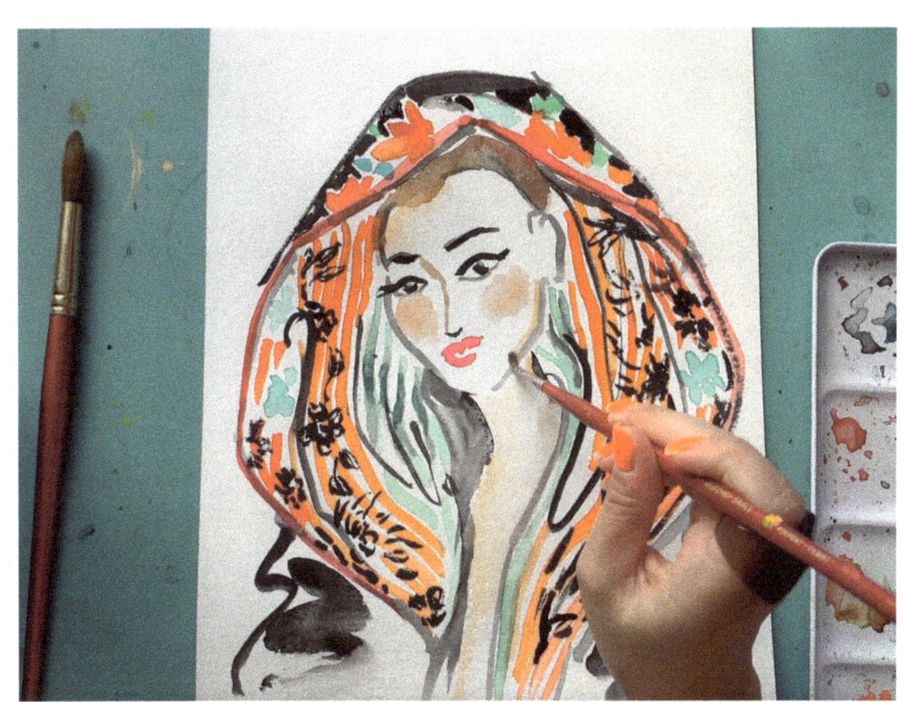

Finish up
the painting
by adding
flesh tone
and shading.

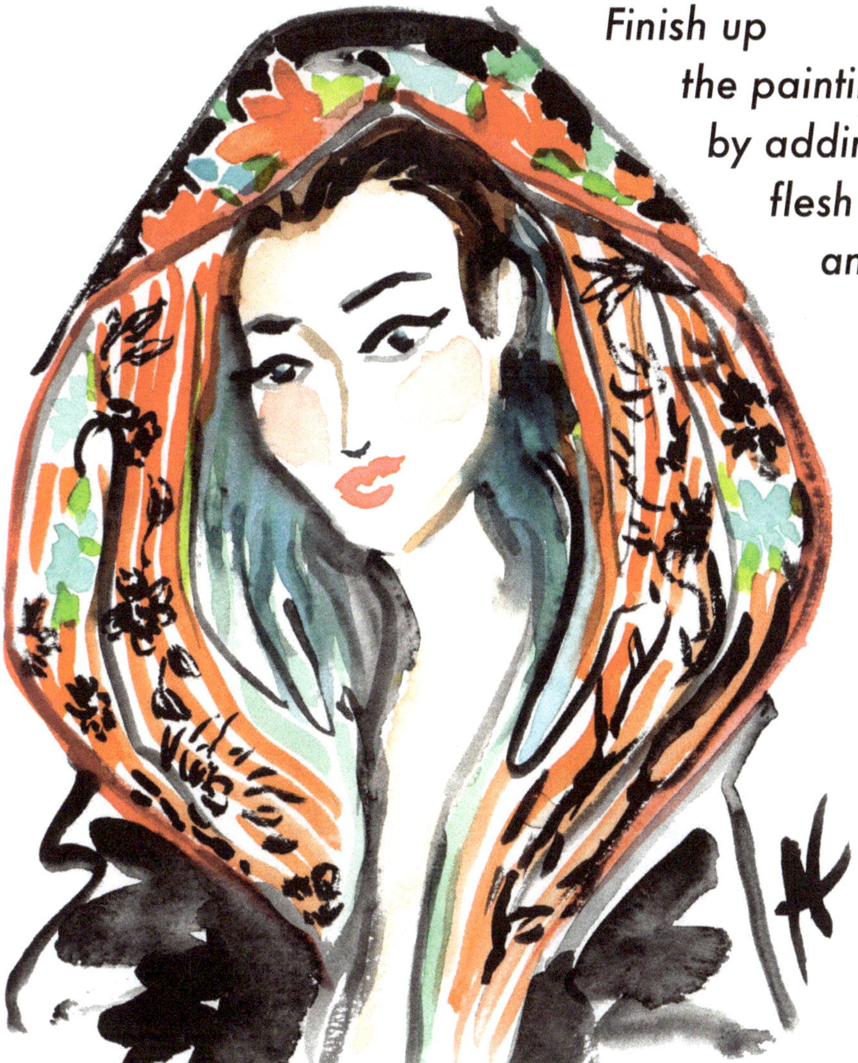

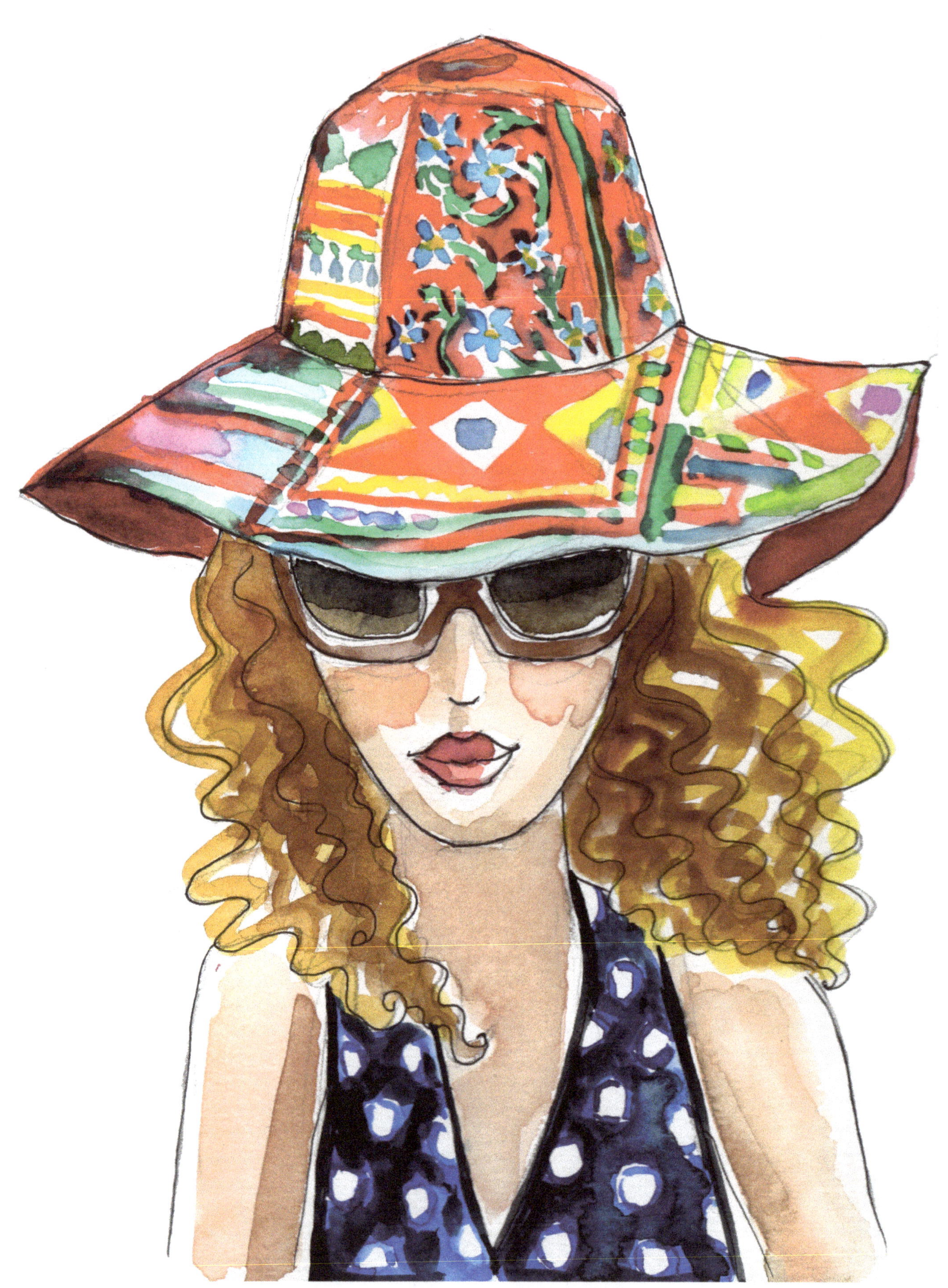

Girl in a Patchwork Hat

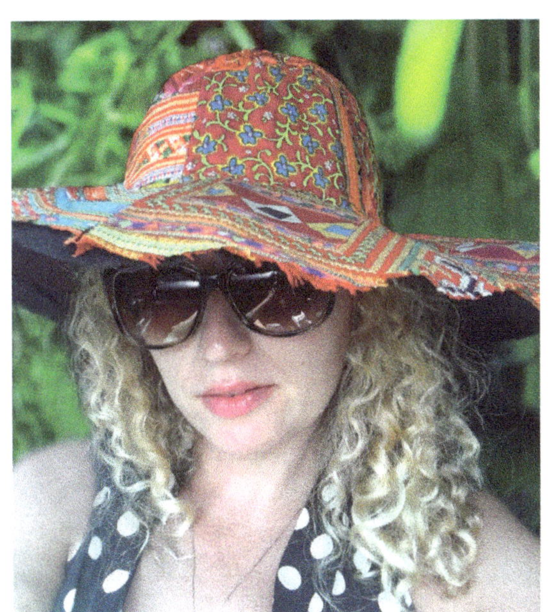

Let's draw and paint a girl in a hat from a photograph.
Sketch the portrait using a pencil.
You can then outline it with a pen.
Even though the photo is cropped, we can finish the hat's sides.

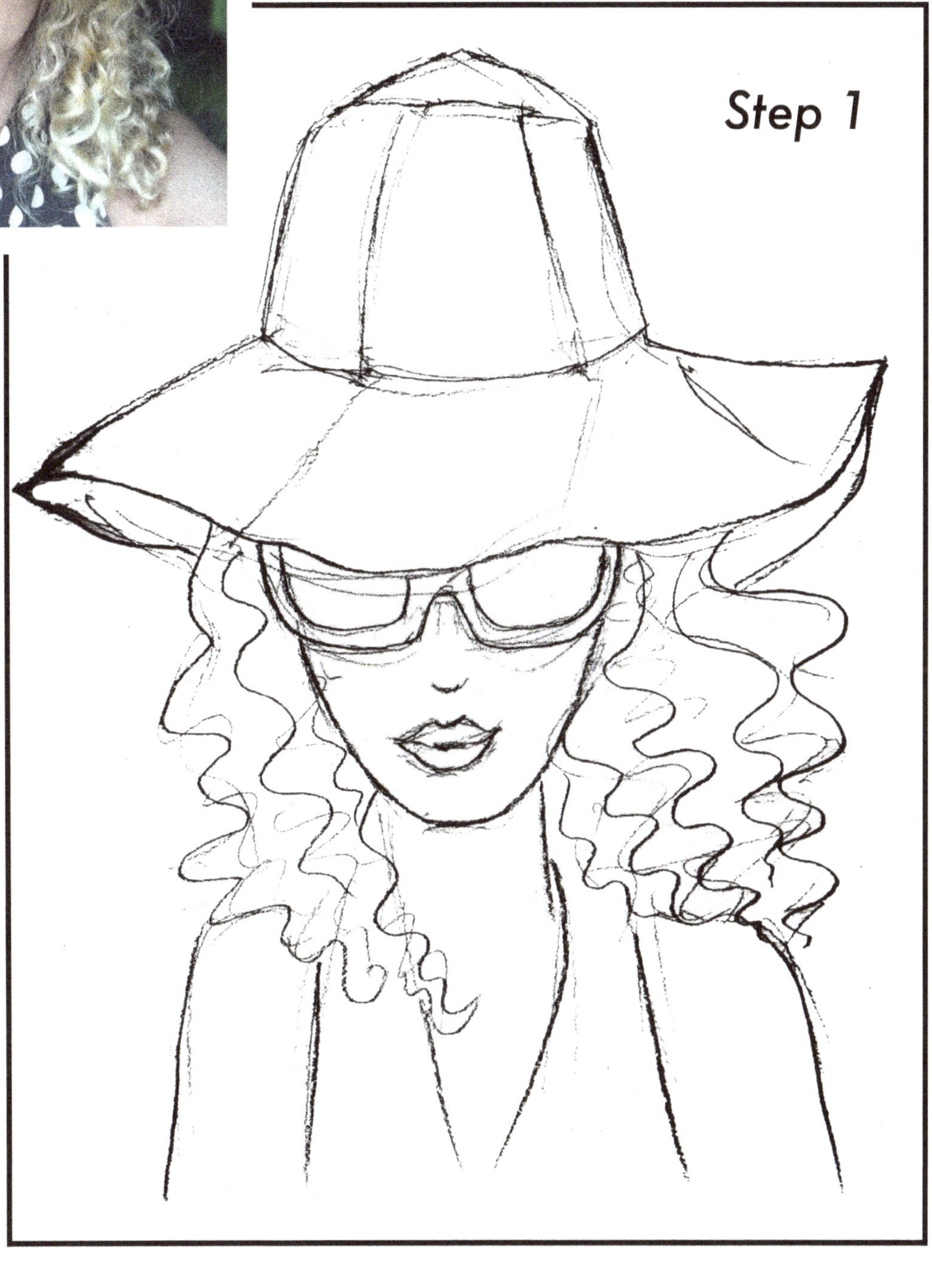

Step 1

Now it's time to paint. Have fun with the pattern of the hat.
You don't need to copy it exactly, but portray the impression of
the hat, as you see it. Use vibrant colors and let them bleed
in places to create that fresh watercolor look.

Step 2

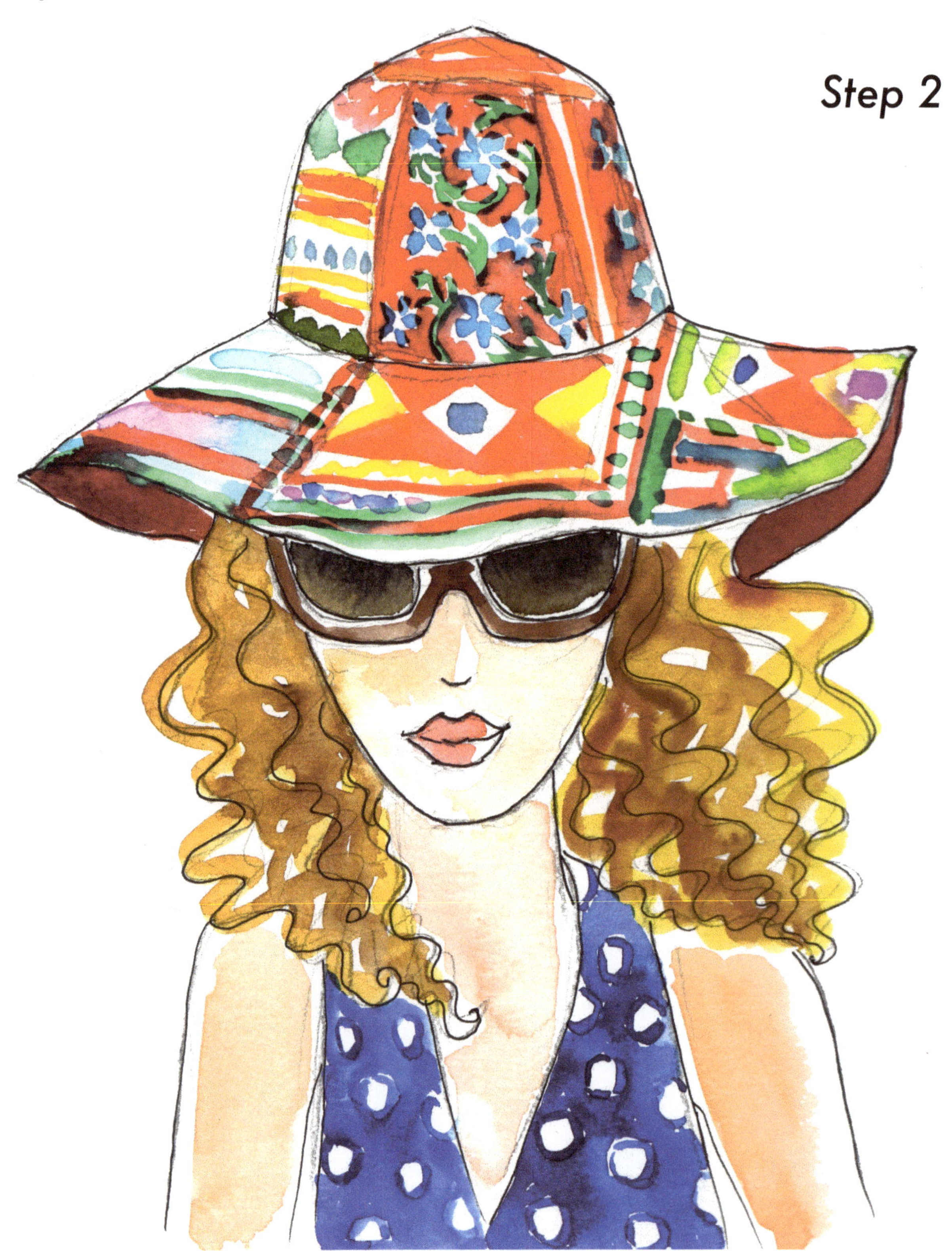

Once the first layer has dried, you can apply more layers. Indicate shadows around the face and body. Add more dimension to the hat and hair.

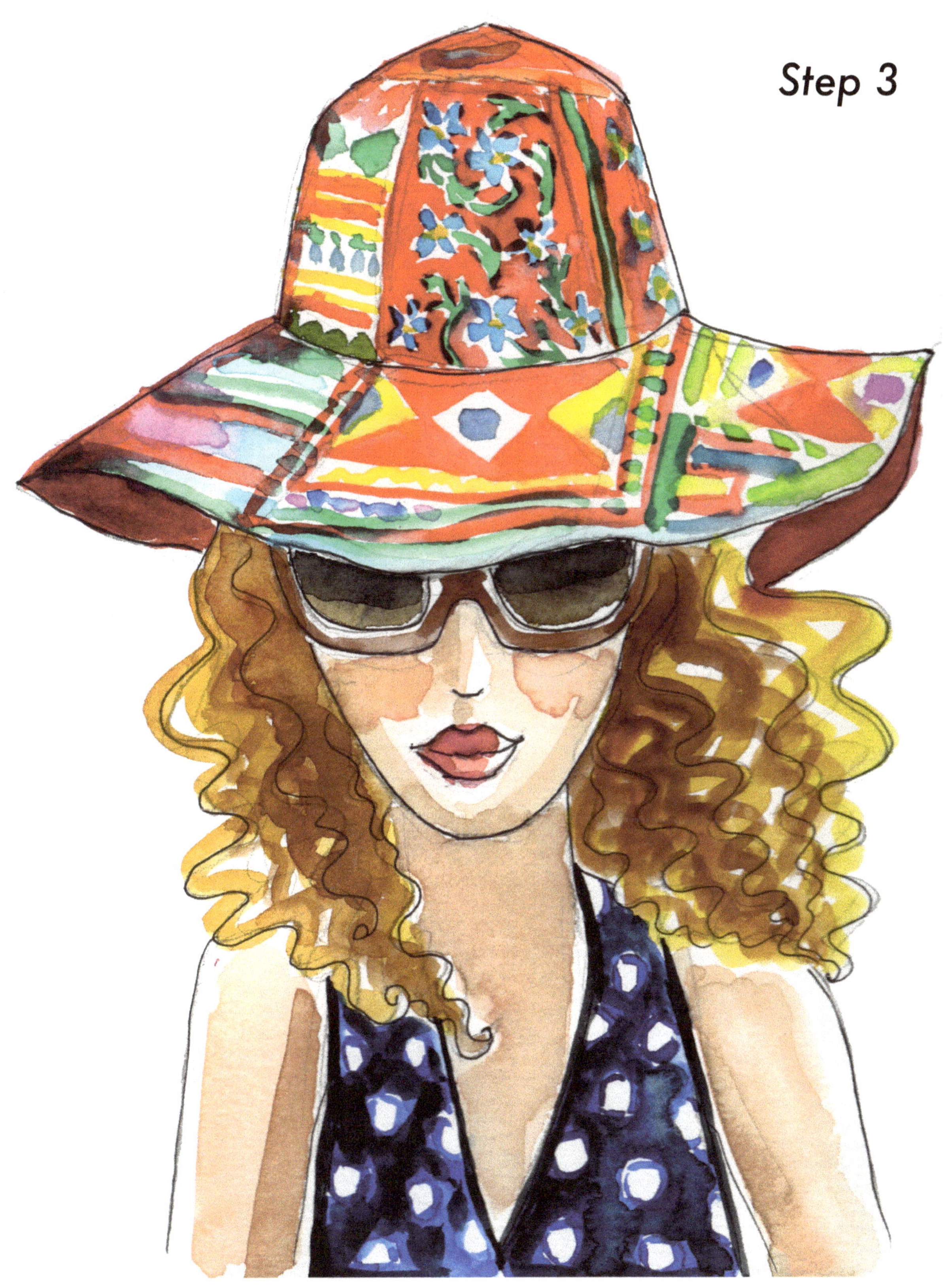

Step 3

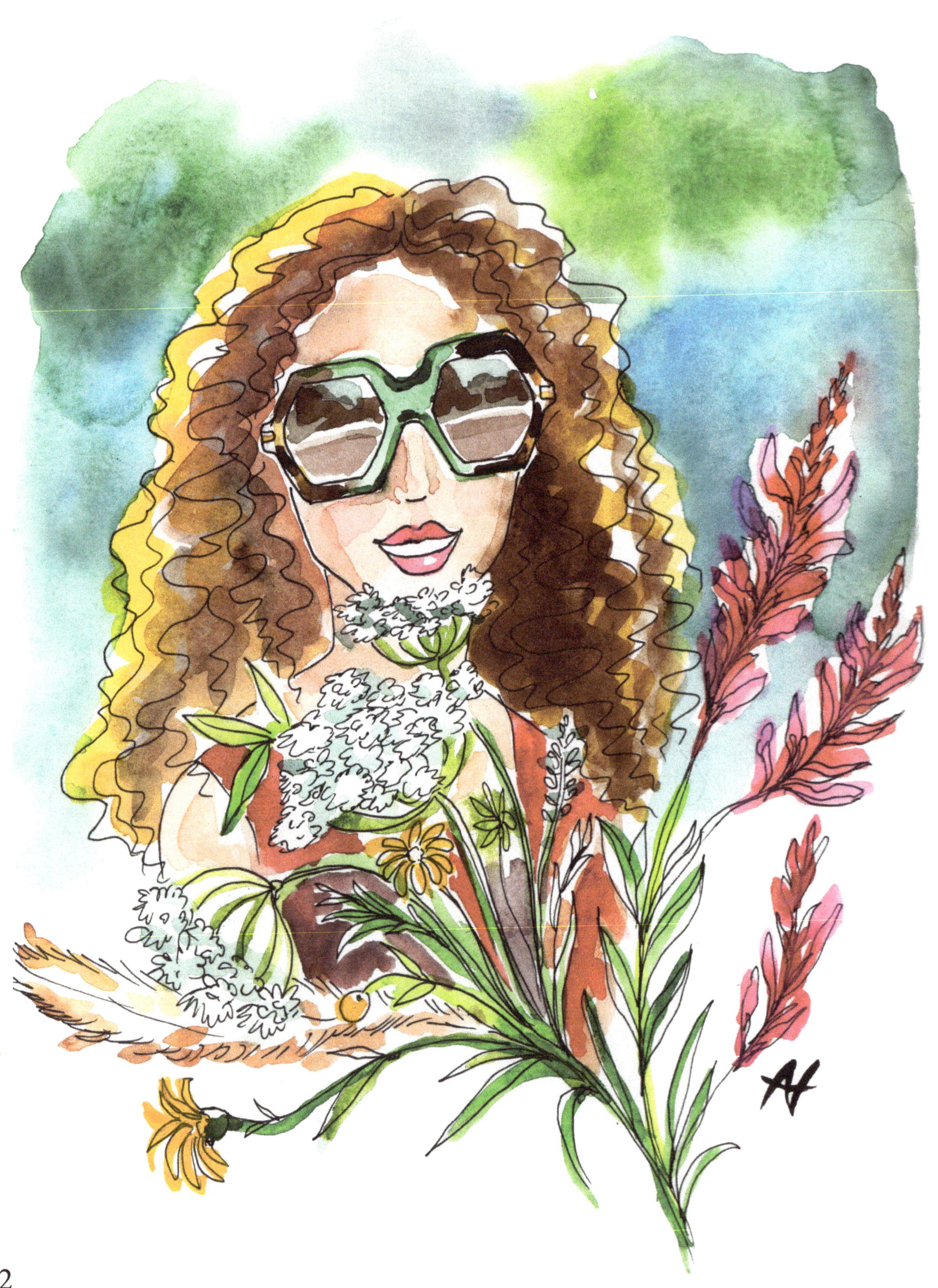

Wild Flower Girl

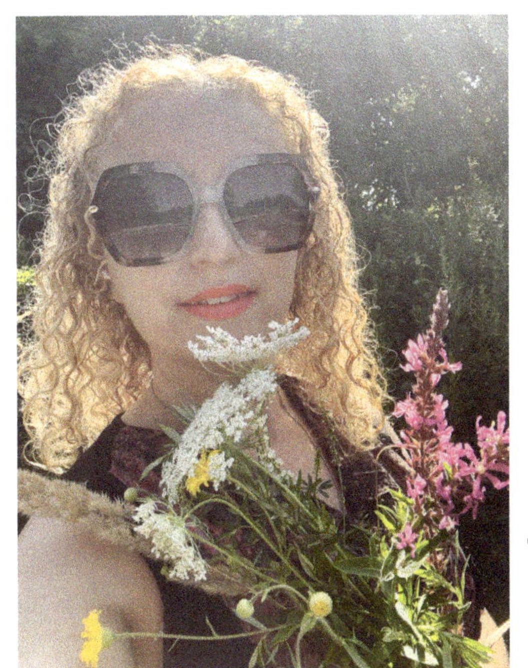

Let's draw and paint a wild flower girl from a photograph.
Sketch the portrait using a pencil, then outline it with a pen and erase the pencil lines.
You can go into the flower and leaf details with your pens.

Step 1

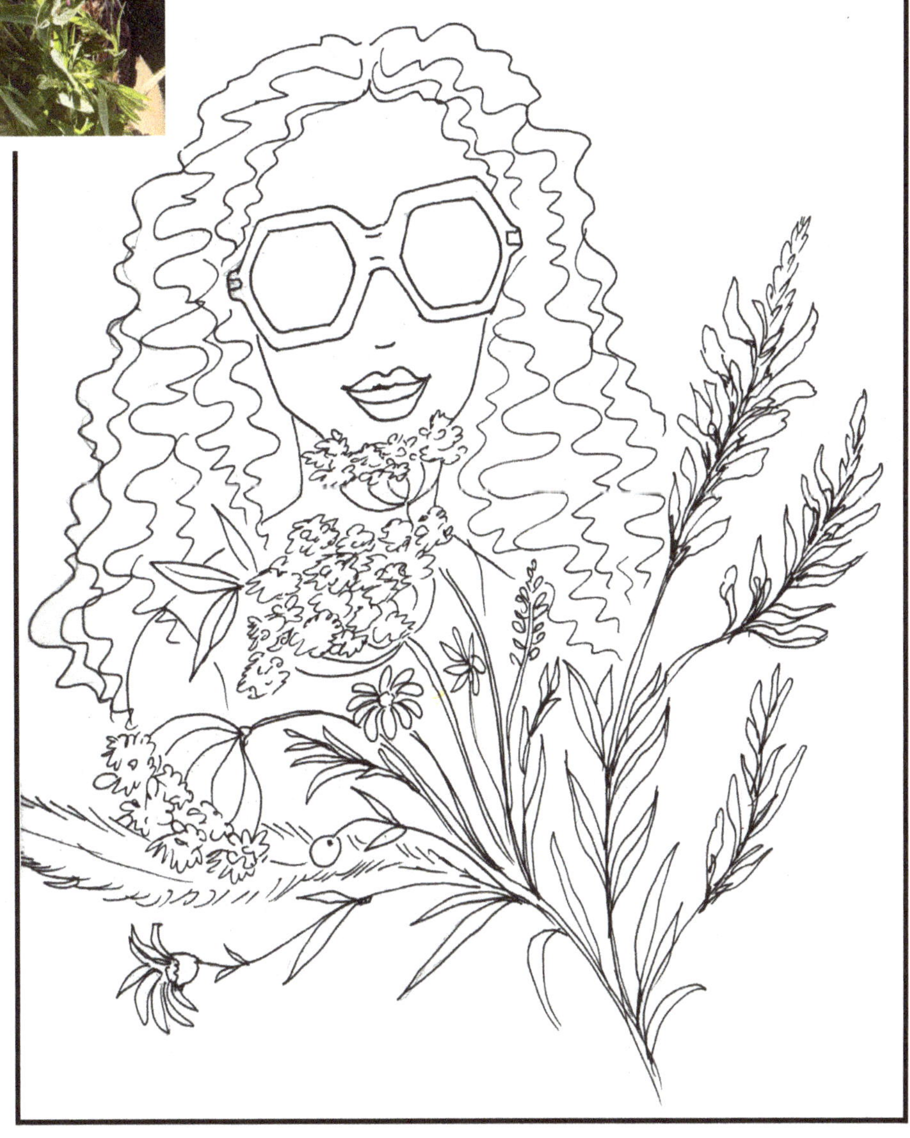

Now apply a layer of watercolor. Let colors run into one another, such as in the hair, flowers, leaves and clothes. Dab off extra water or color where you wish.

Step 2

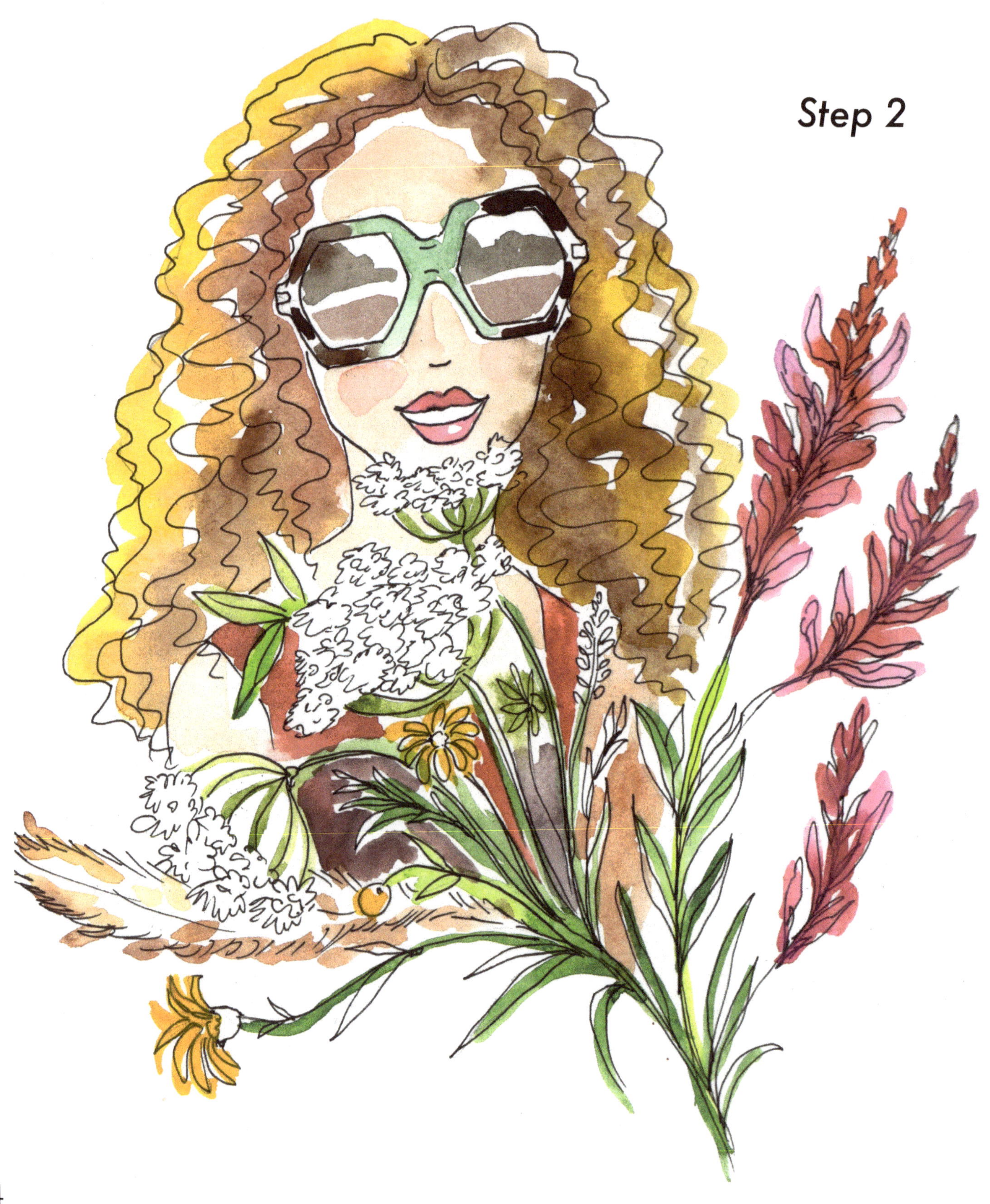

Once that watercolor layer has dried, we can apply more watercolor. Pay attention to details on the sunglasses and hair. You can also add a nice blurry watercolor background. Play with colors running into each other here.

Step 3

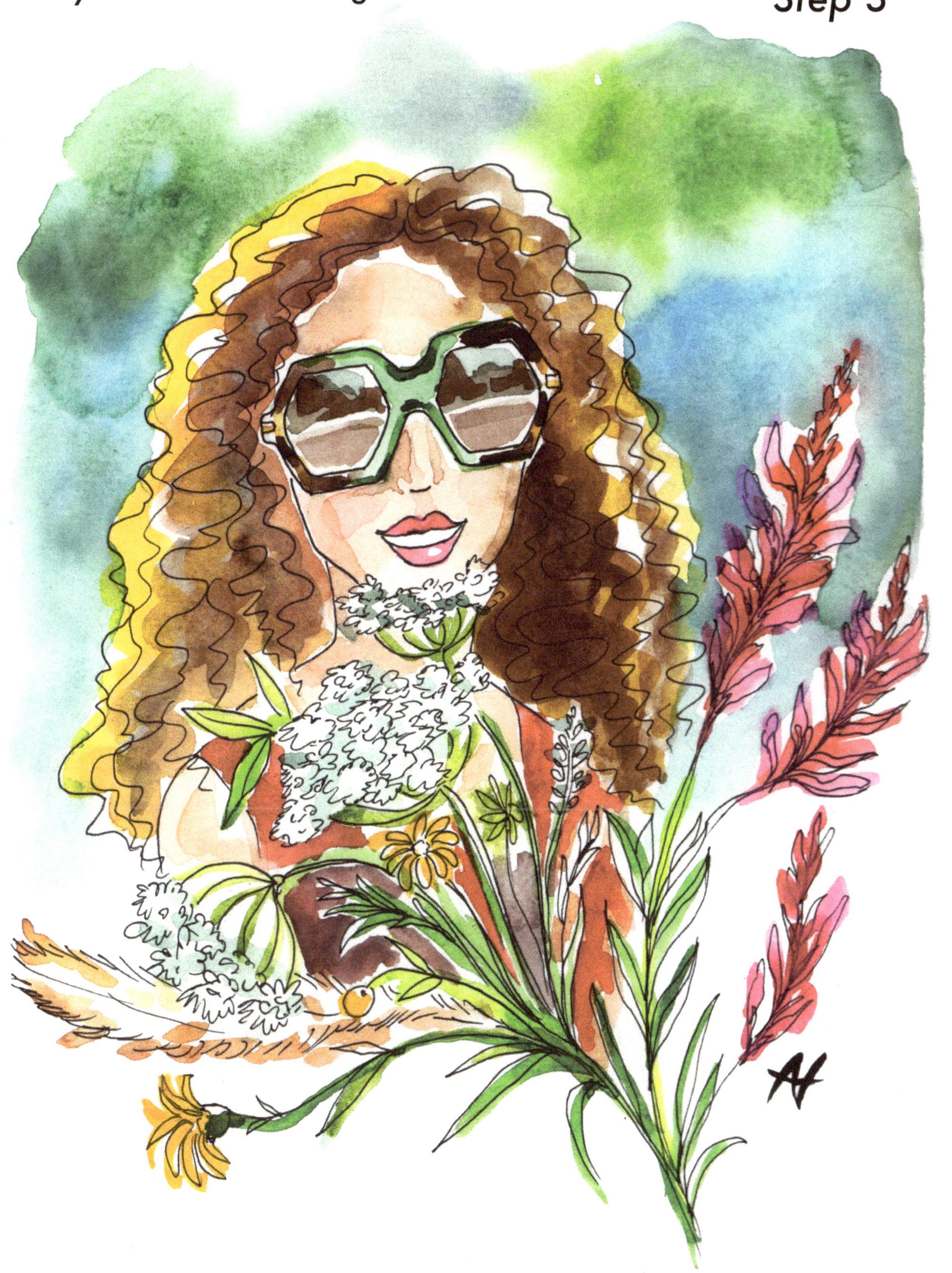

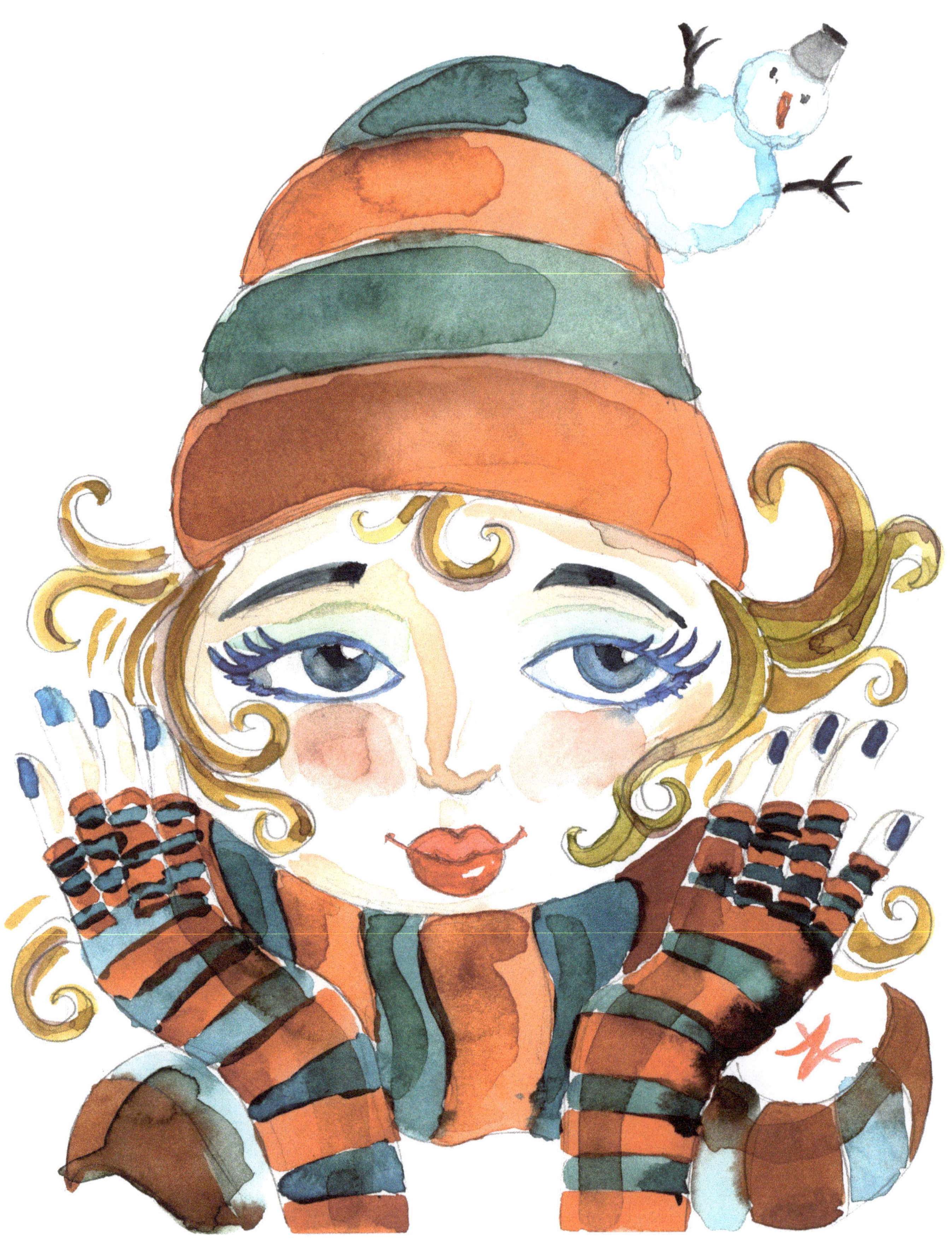

Winter Time Girl

The next series of portraits are more whimsical. Once we master painting from photos, we can explore creating more imaginative face illustrations in watercolor. Sketch this winter girl illustration.

Step 1

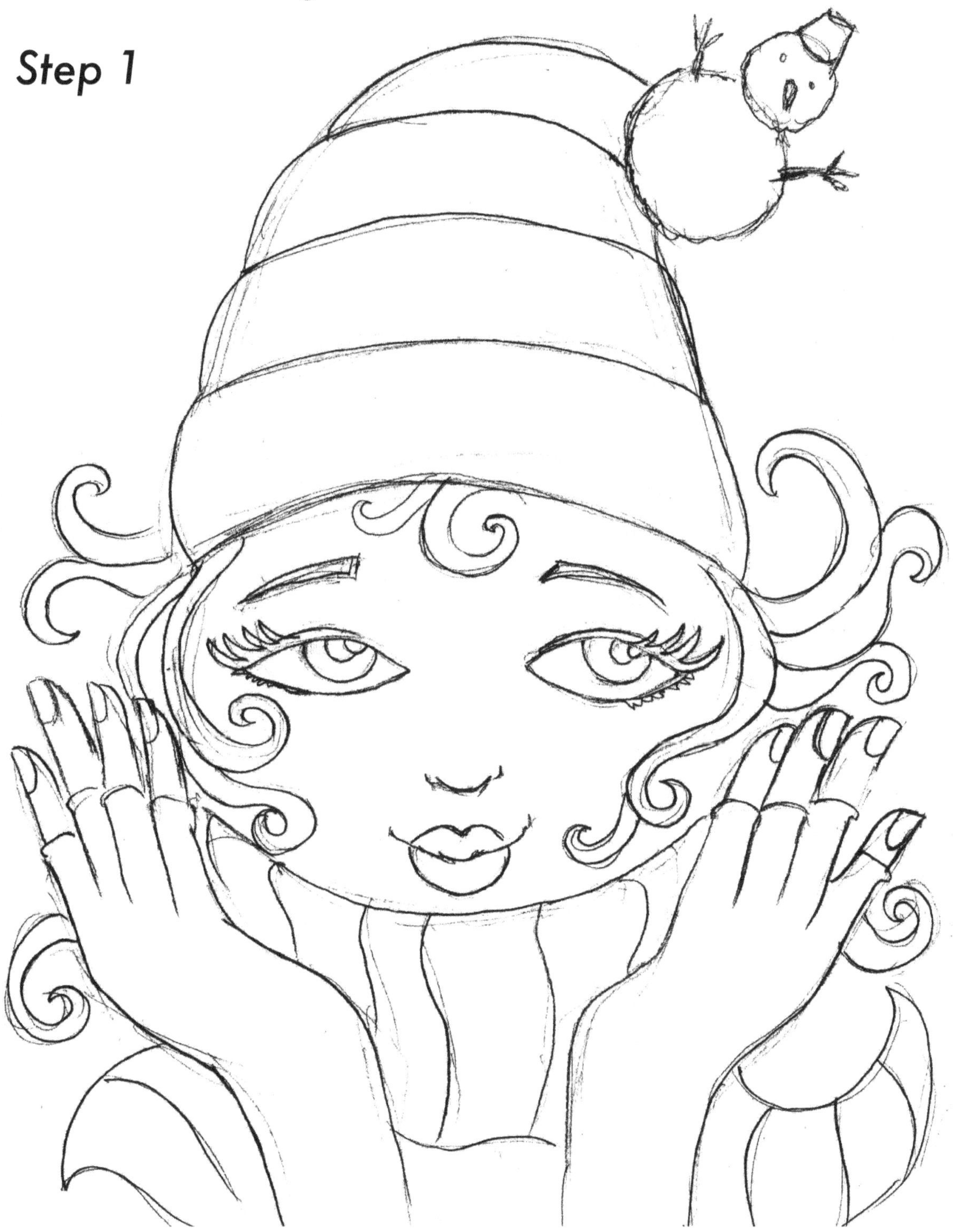

For this illustration, let's use teal and orange shades of watercolor to create the hat, gloves and scarf. Note the way the lines follow the shapes of the hands, head and neck. Use light blue for shading on the snowman. Indicate hair and facial features.

Step 2

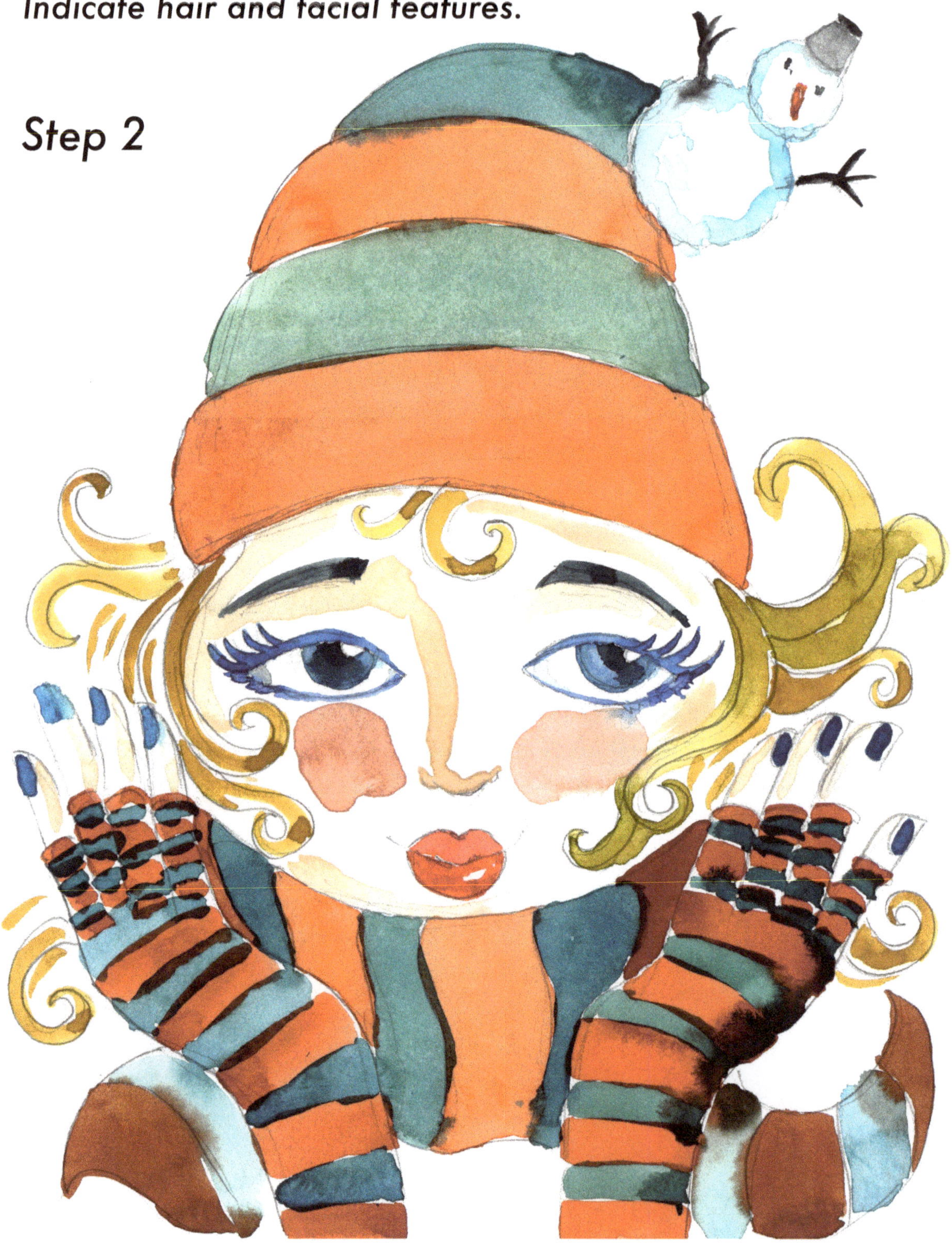

Once the first layer dries, apply shading where you wish,
for a more finished look. Keep it fresh, do not overwork.
If you need to correct any colors, you can wet the paintbrush
and lightly rub it on the color to take it off, then you can
blot it with a tissue.

Step 3

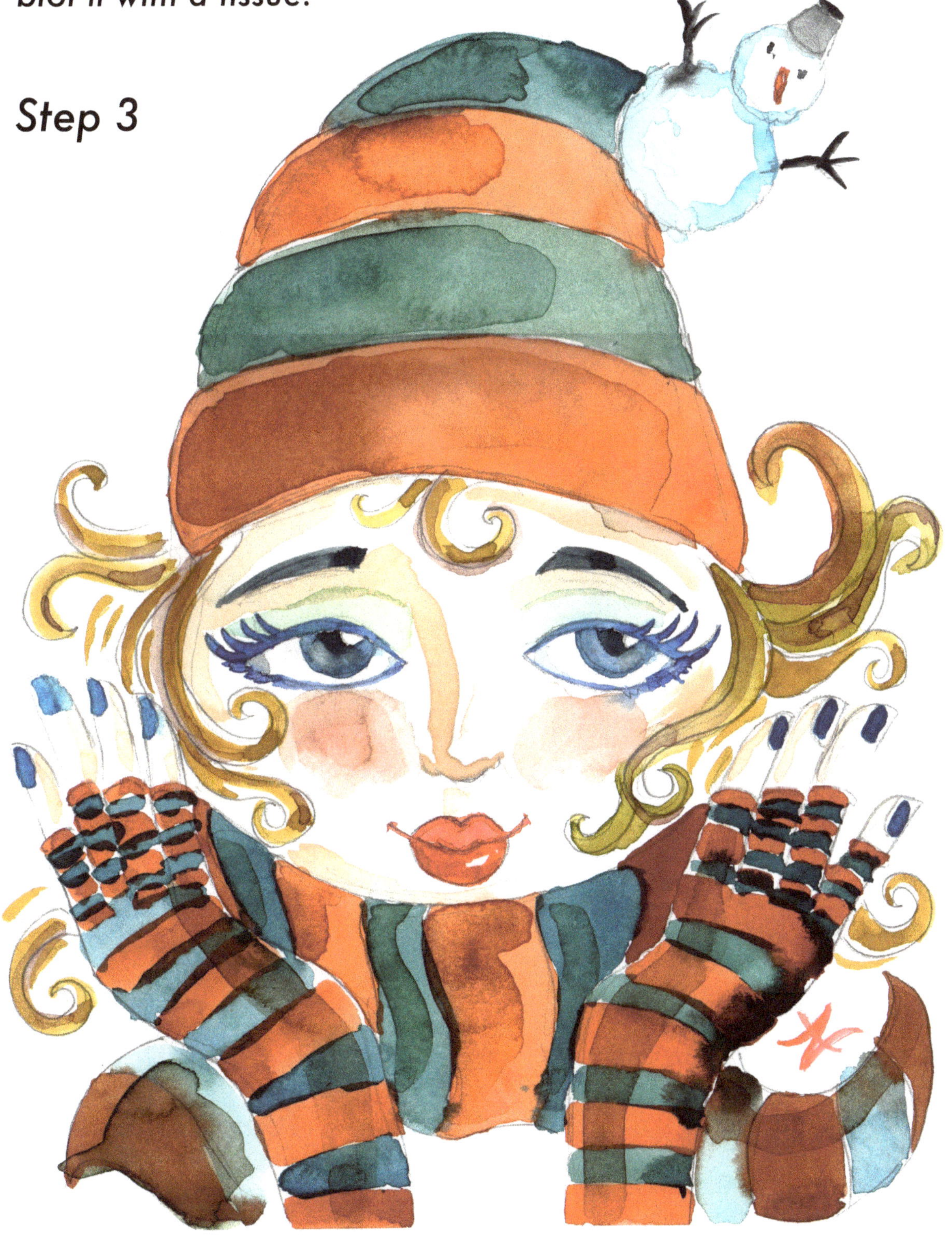

Bird Girl

This whimsical portrait features a girl with branches for hair, with birds sitting on the branches. We can also see a part of her wrap, which resembles a nest. Sketch out the illustration as you see it here, using a pencil.

Step 1

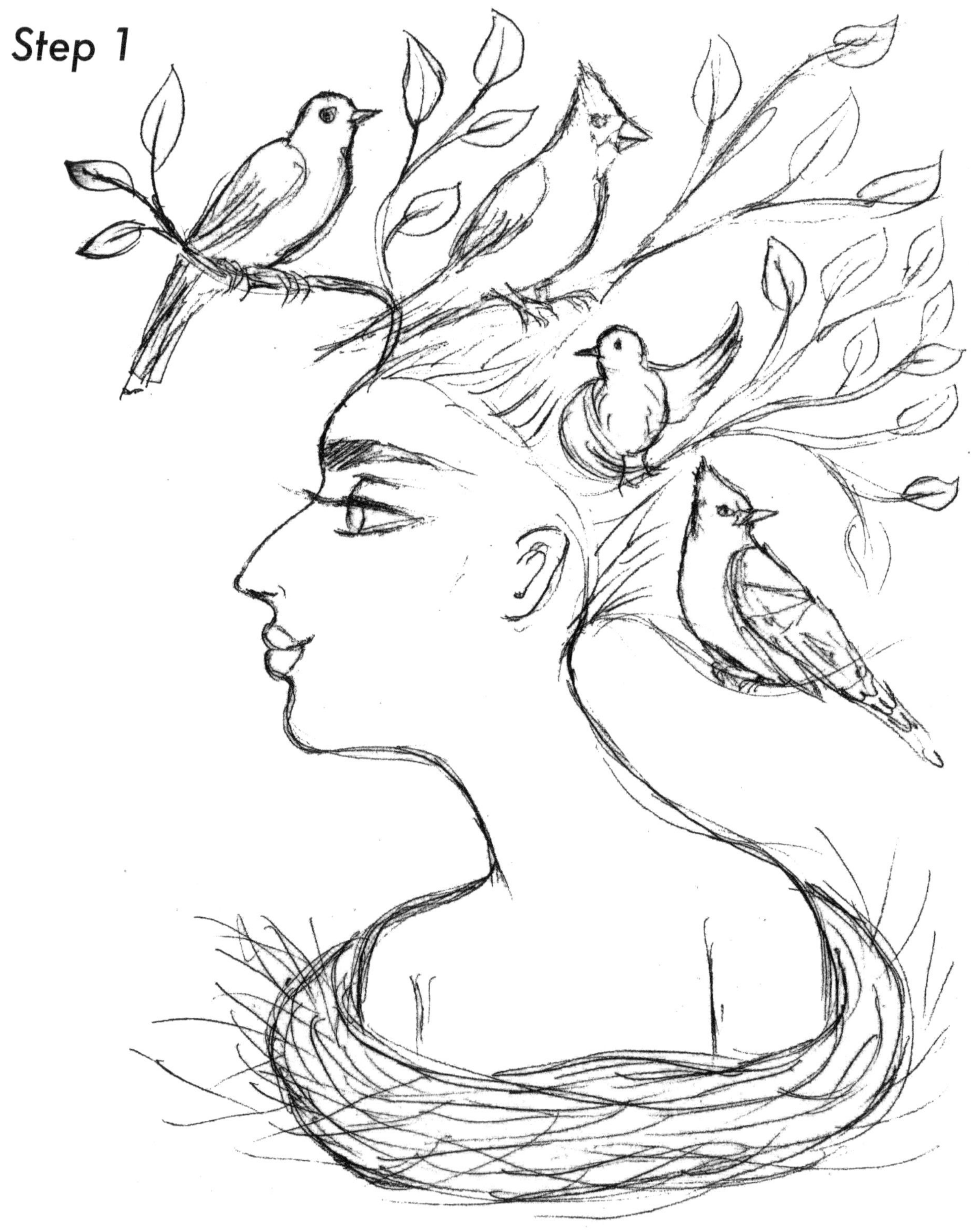

For this illustration, I chose to outline it with artist pens. Using a medium thickness pen, outline your sketch. Choose the lines you wish to outline, and erase any extra lines after you are done.

Step 2

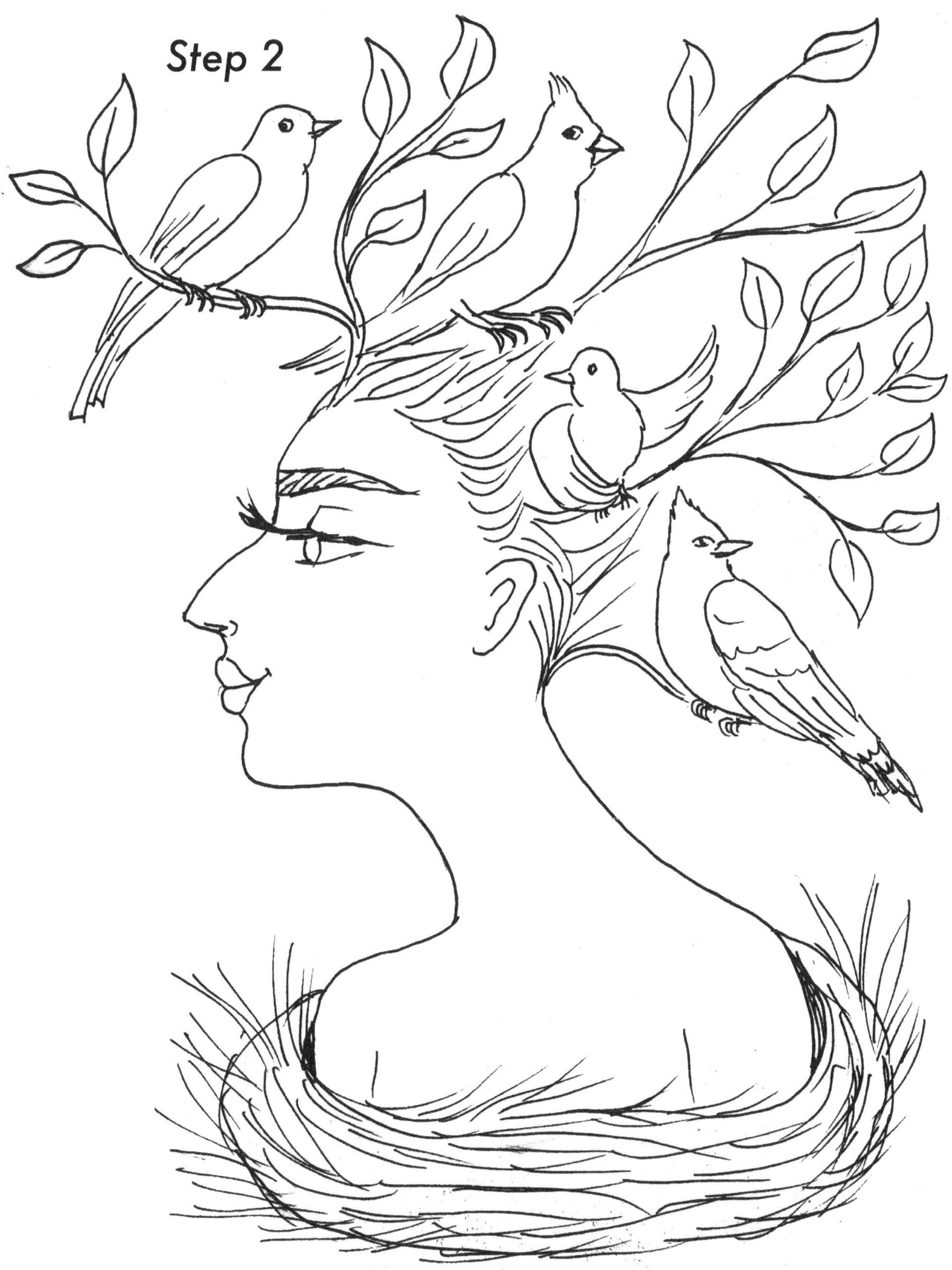

Now, apply your first watercolor layer. Leave the white of the paper in certain spots, where you wish the light to fall.

Step 3

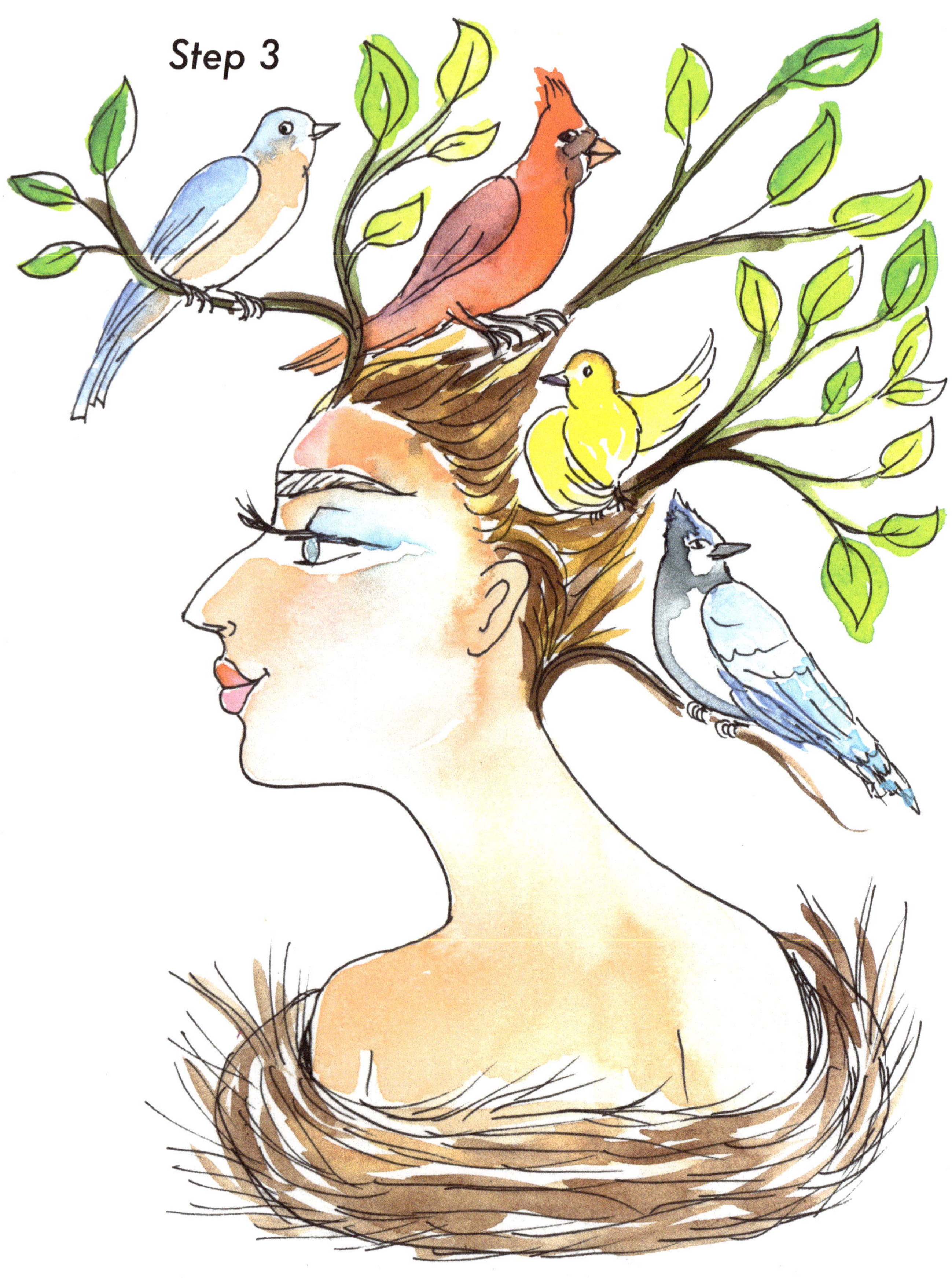

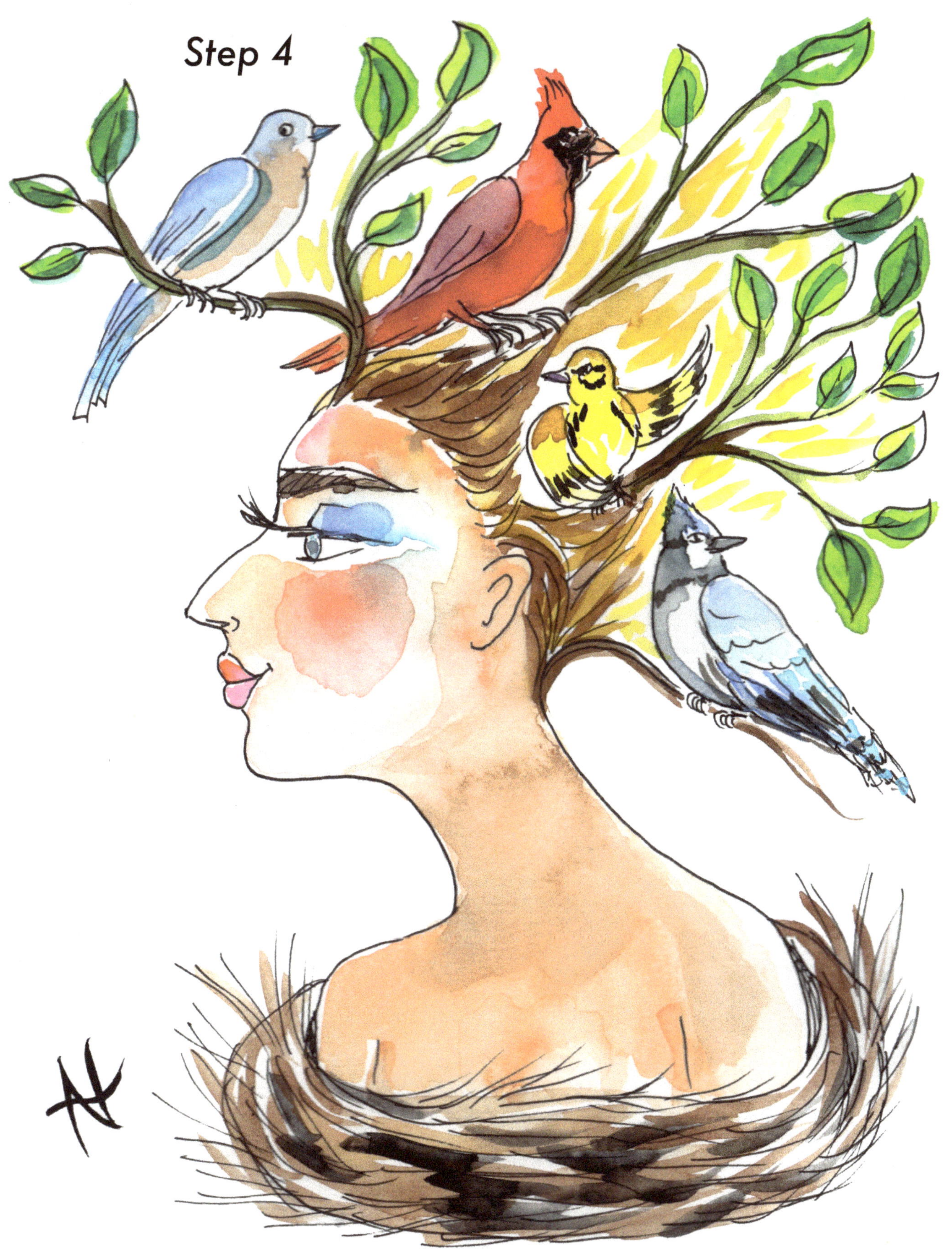

Finally, finish up the portrait by adding your top layer as you see here.
Add shading, dimension, fill in some areas between branches.

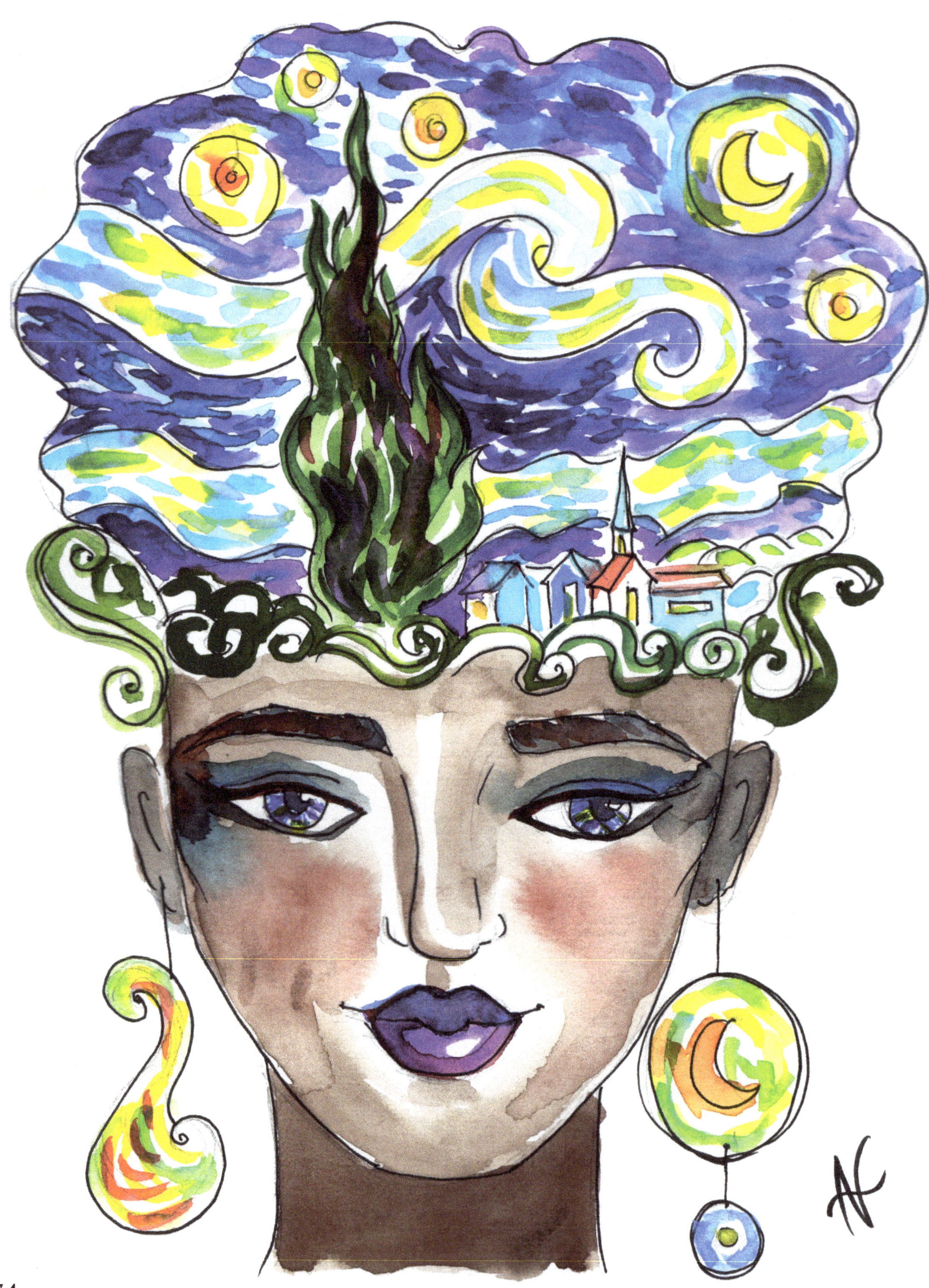

Starry Night Girl

For this exercise, let's create a girl inspired by Vincent Van Gogh's painting - "Starry Night." She will have the images from the painting incorporated into her hair. Sketch out the concept, then outline it.

Step 1

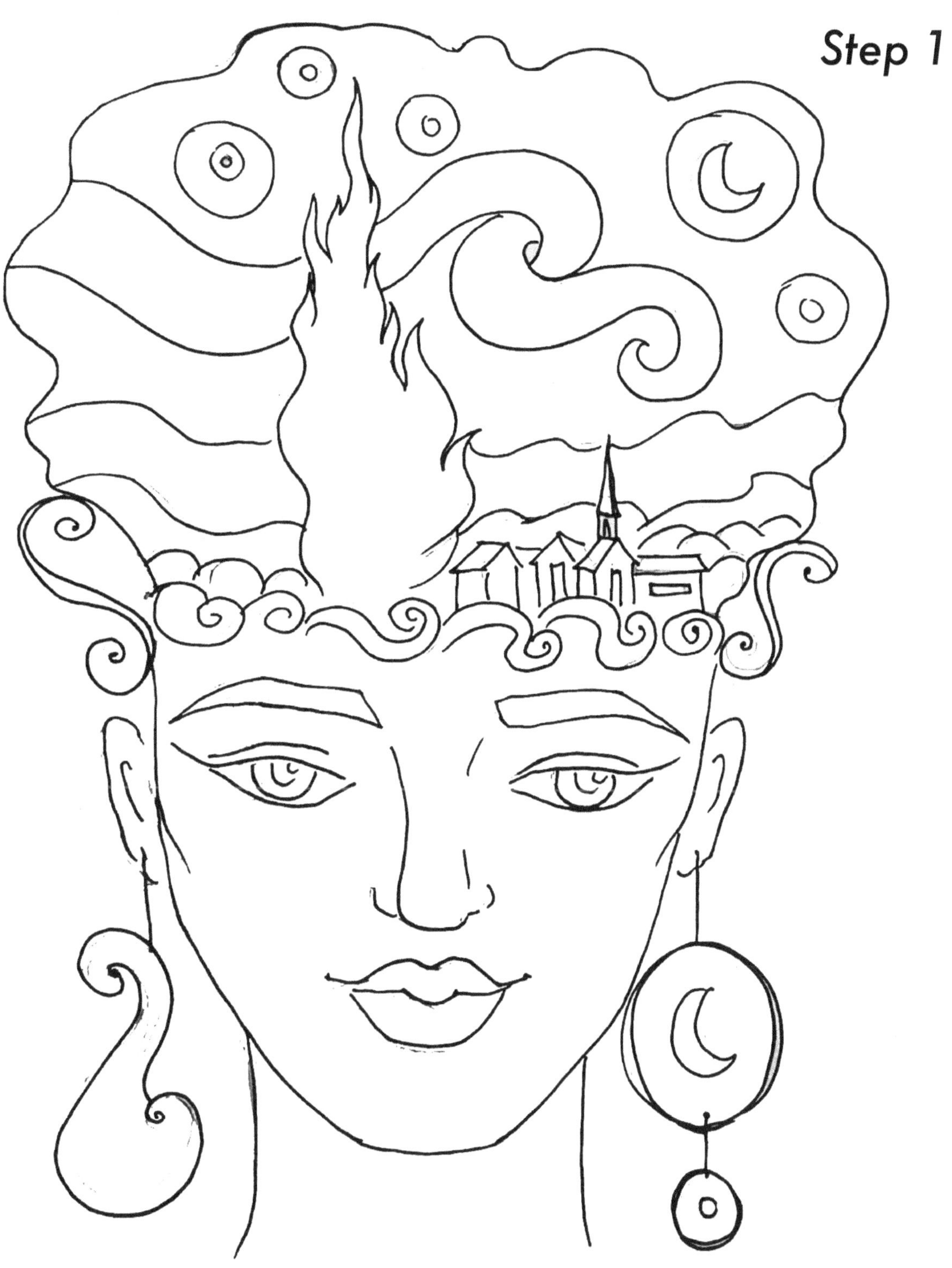

Now let's apply watercolor. We are going to mimic the strokes Van Gogh used in his painting. They follow the objects to create a sense of movement. Apply skin tone and dramatic makeup to match the hair.

Step 2

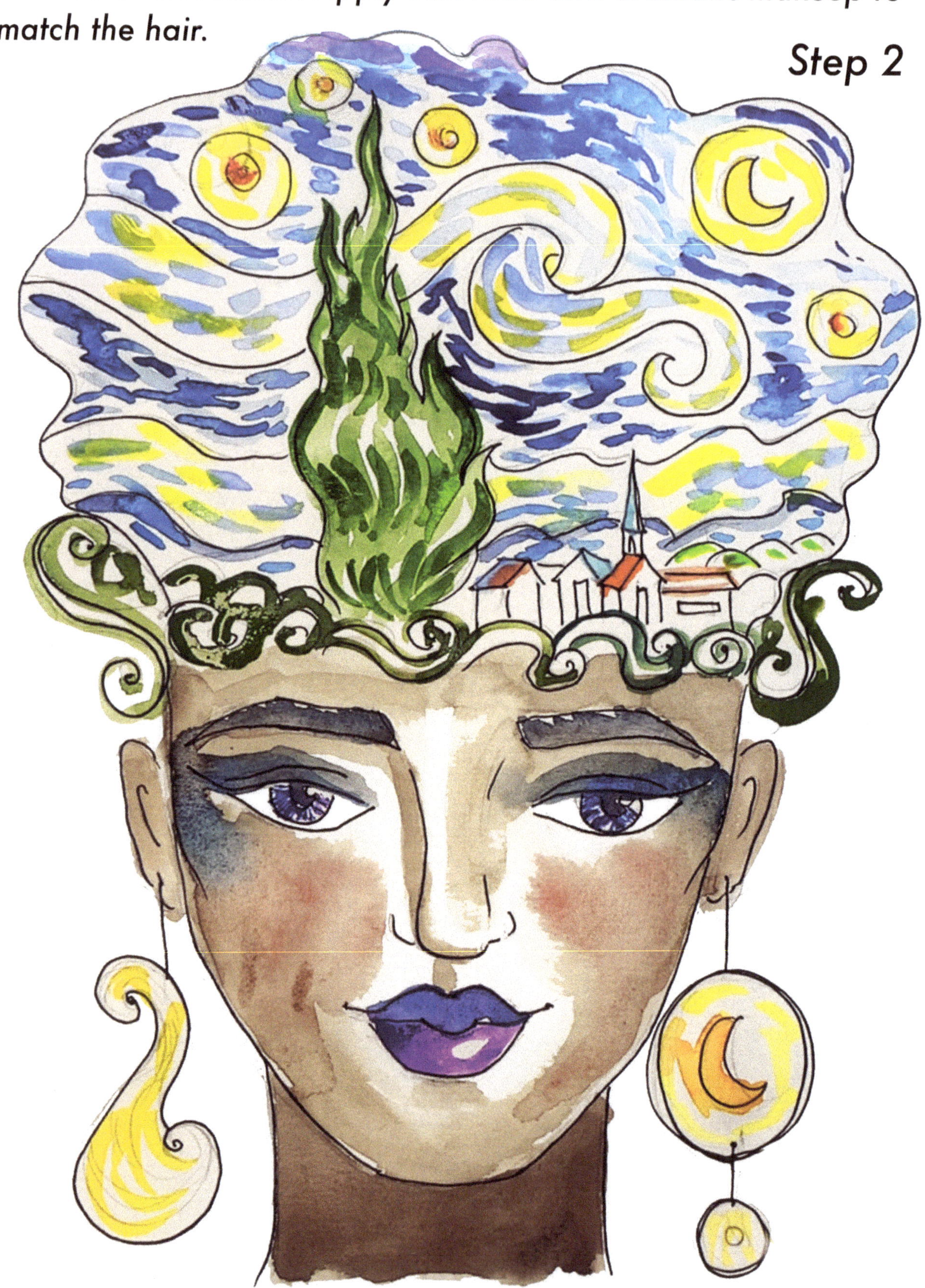

Once that layer dries, add final touches, shading and colors.

Step 3

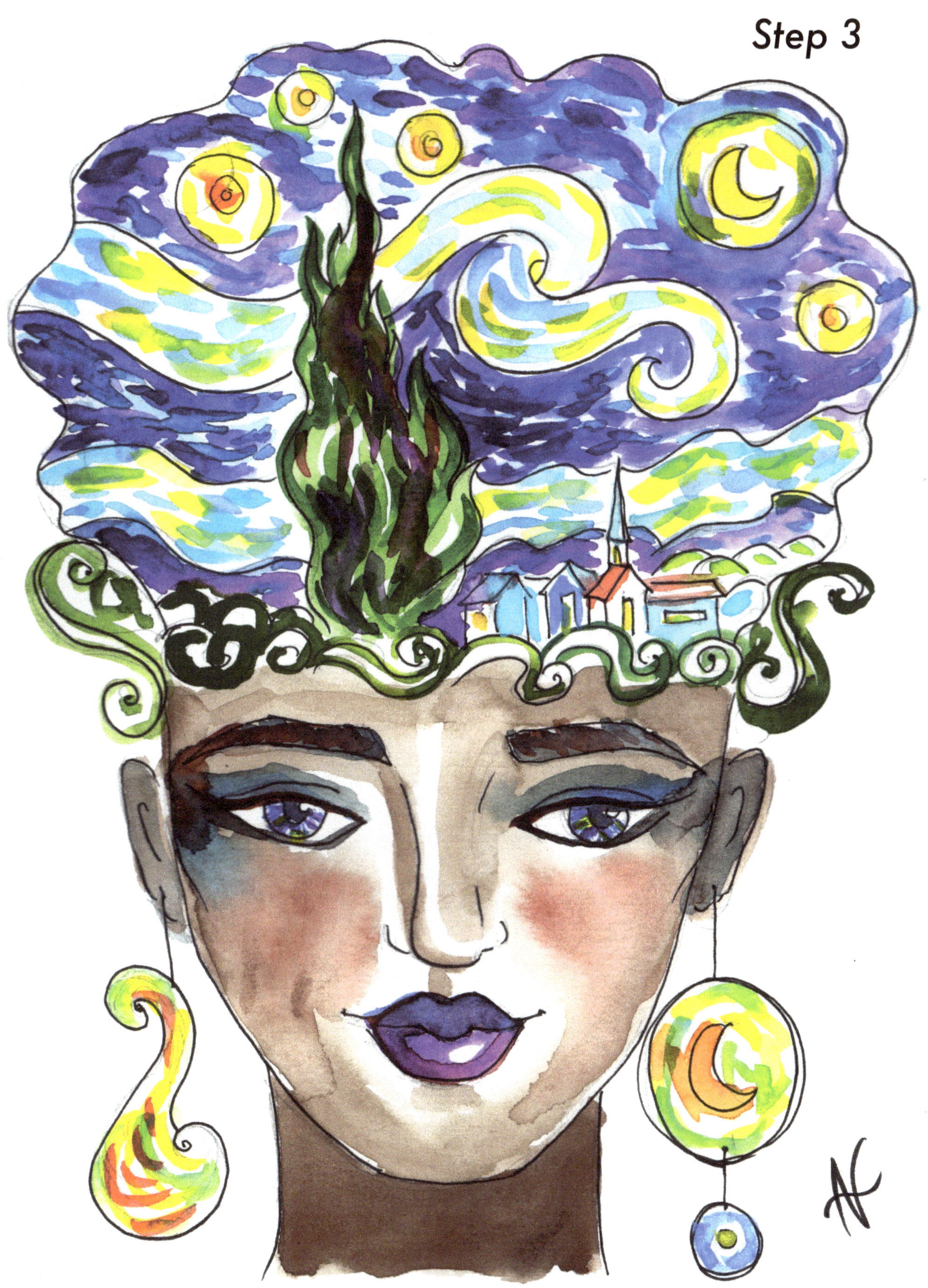

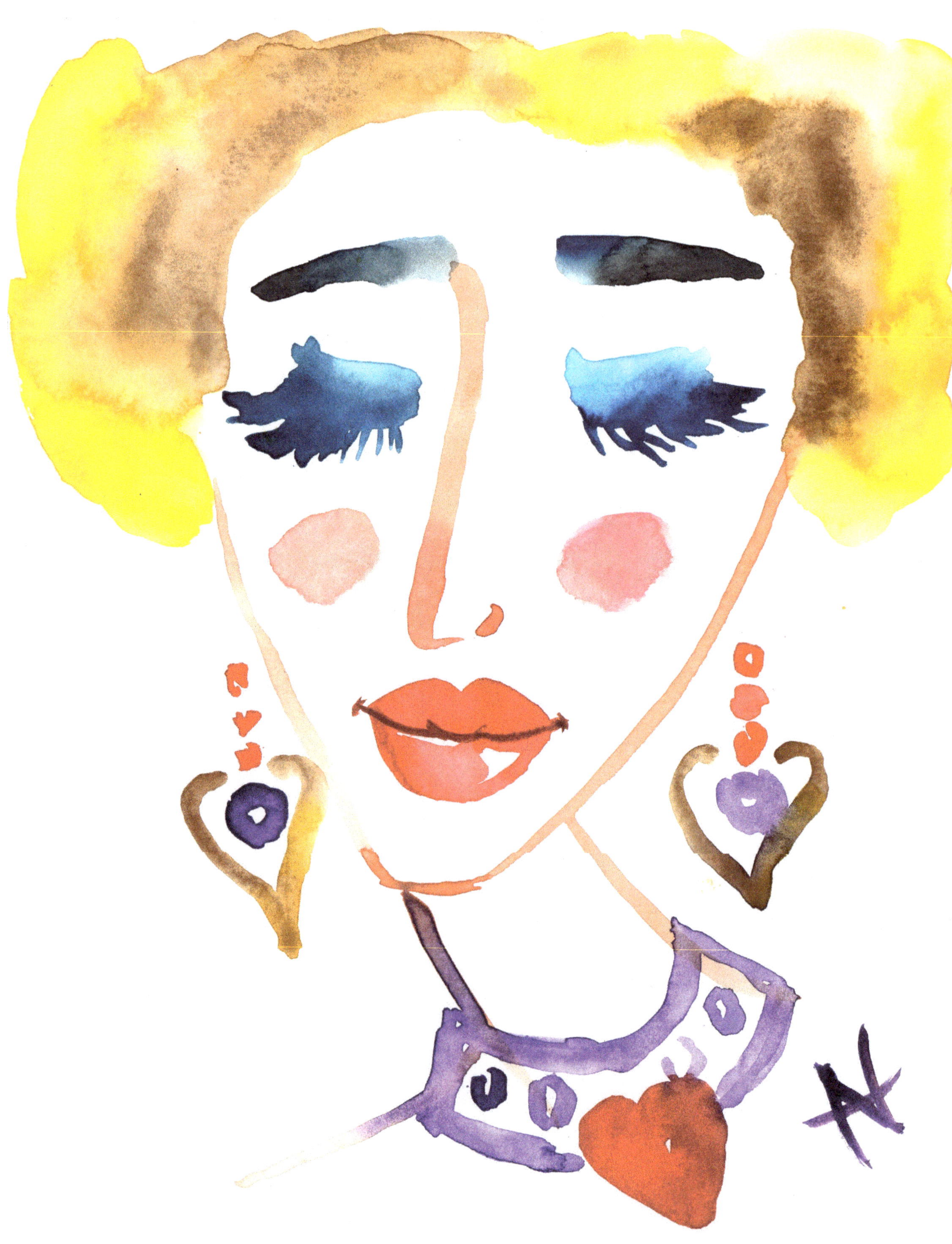

Loose Watercolor Face

For our last exercise, let's create a stylized and expressive watercolor face illustration. We will use straight watercolor for this portrait. Start with painting the eyes. Vary the shades of blue for the lashes and eyebrows. Let colors bleed into one another.

Step 1

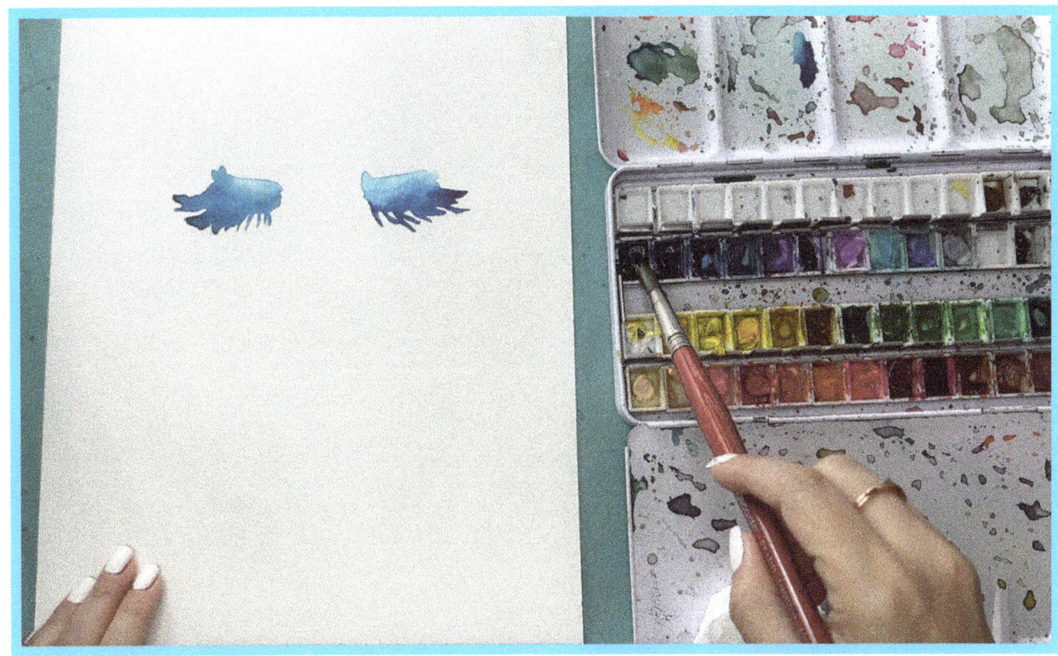

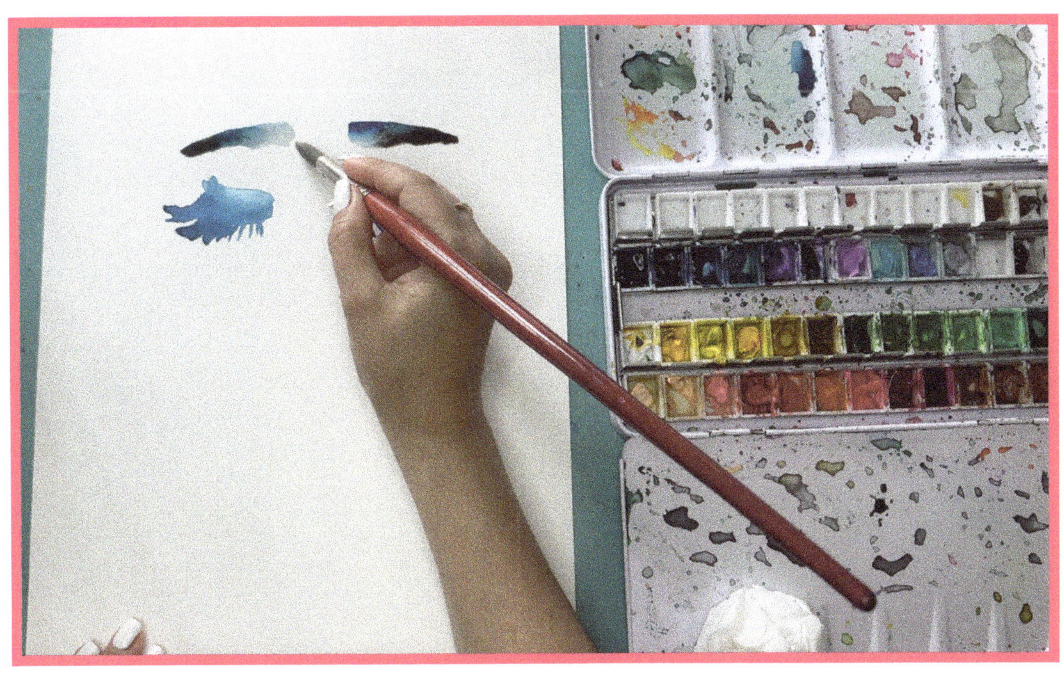

Now paint the nose, lips, the outline for the face and hair. Use analogous color shades for the skin/nose outline, lips and hair to create beautiful watercolor blends.

Step 2

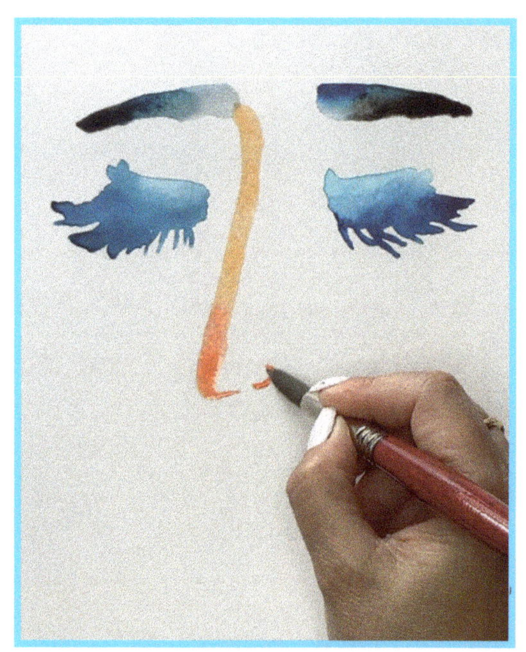

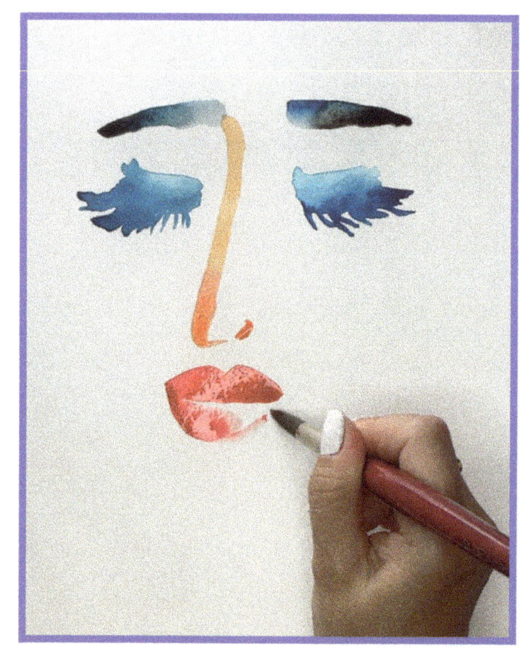

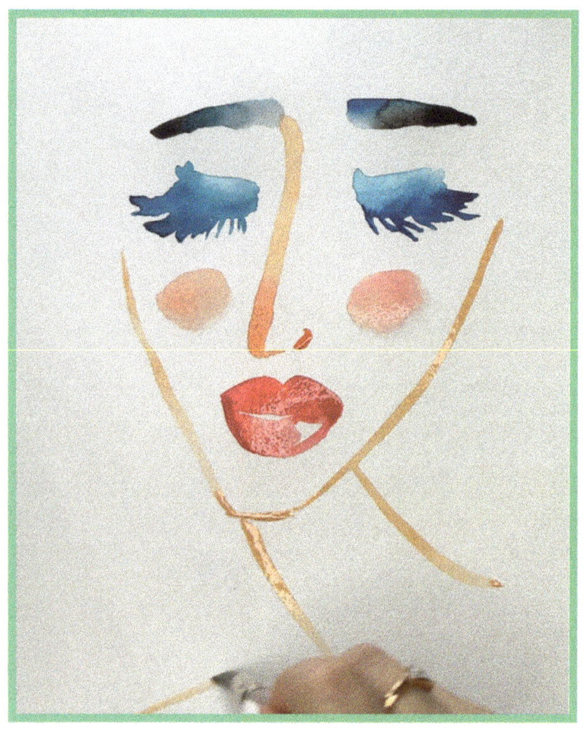

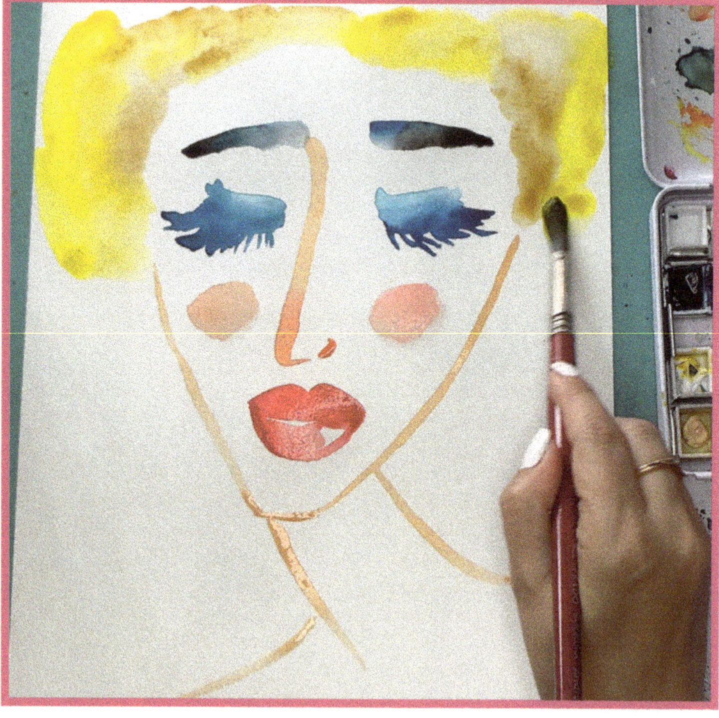

Finally, add in simple accessories, like a necklace and earrings. Now you have created a loose and fun watercolor illustration!

Step 3

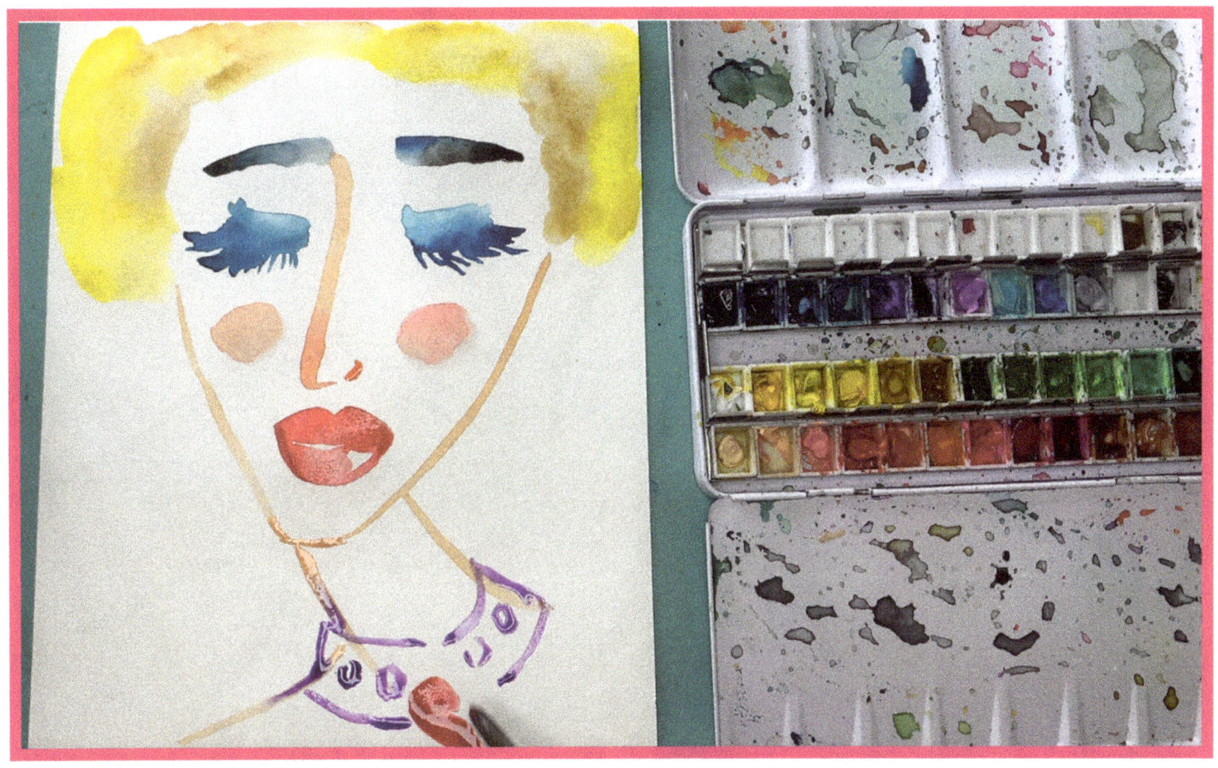

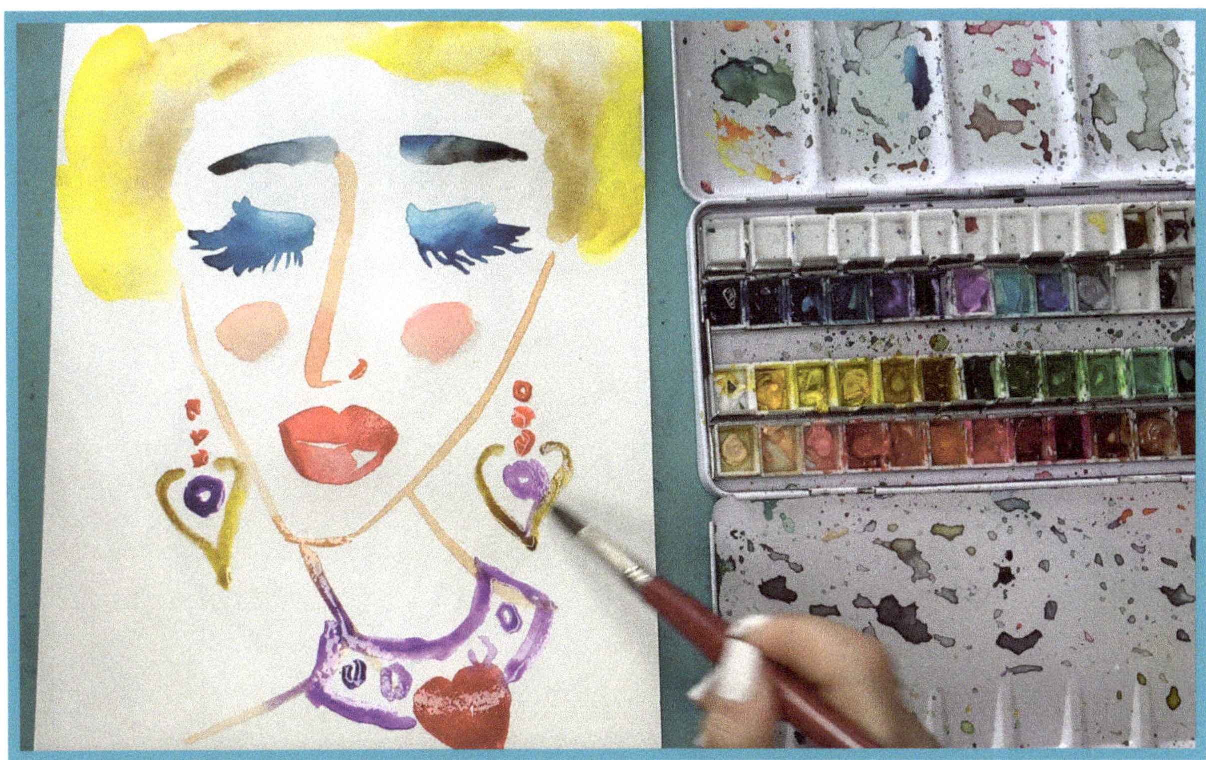

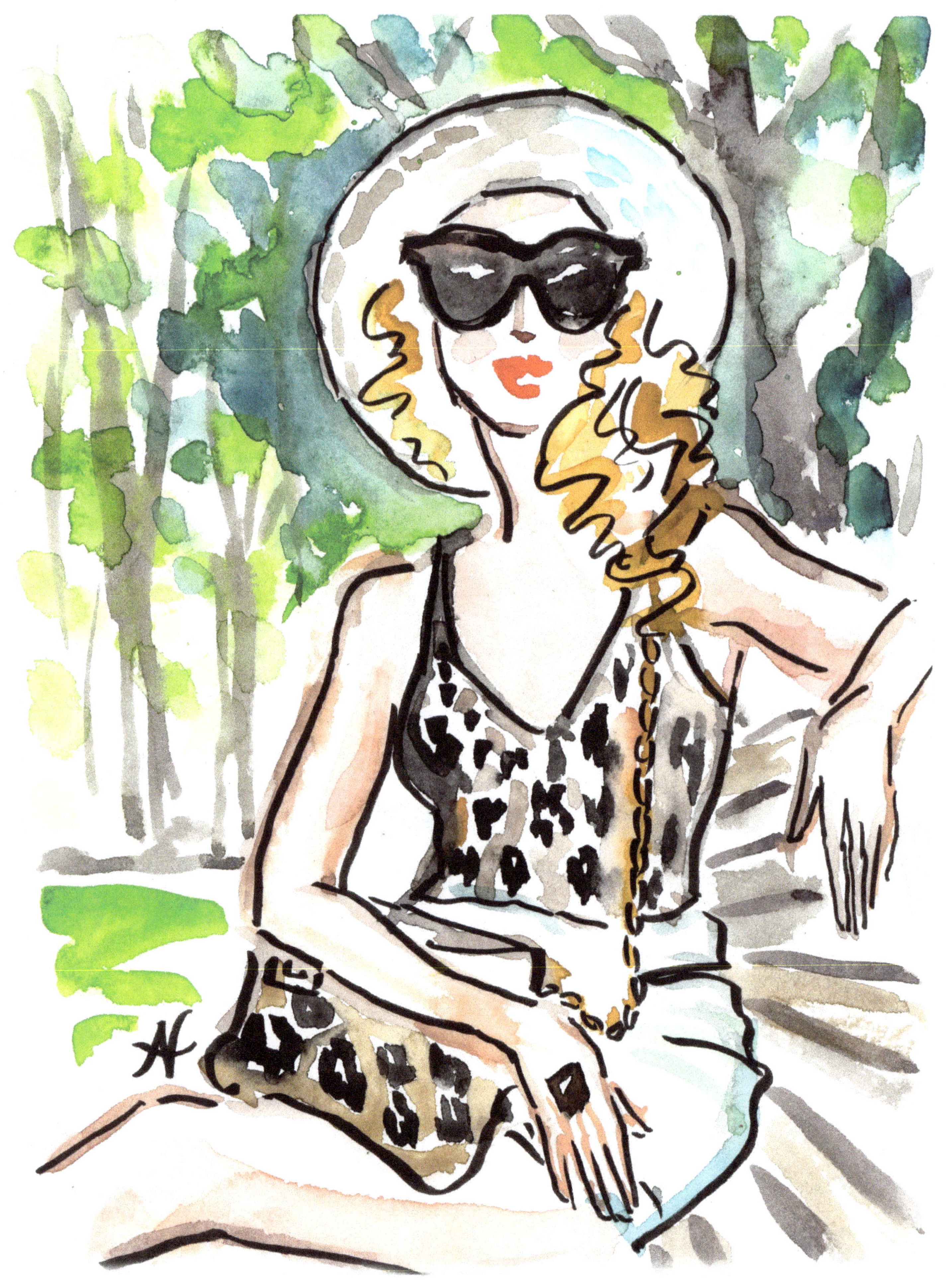

Afterword

Thank you for getting this book!

I sincerely hope that it has inspired you to take creative freedoms on your watercolor journey, while learning something new!

You can share what you created by tagging me on Instagram: @anna_nadler_art

Enjoyed the book? Feel free to leave a review!

Also, check out more books on my website, by scanning the QR code below, or going to: AnnaNadlerArt.com

Thank you!

Anna